CLASSIC

AIRCRAFT

WALTER J. BOYNE

PUBLICATIONS INTERNATIONAL, LTD.

Contents

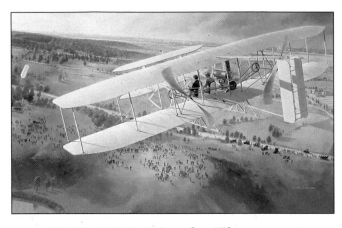

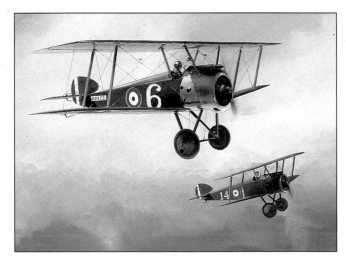

ISBN: 1-56173-464-0

PHOTO CREDITS
John Batchelor: 4 (bottom), 6, 17, 24, 33, 48 (left center), 49 (top), 89 (top left, center), 90 (bottom), 92; **Beech Aircraft Corporation:** 72-73, 74, 75 (top left), 77 (center); Pat Zerbe: 77 (bottom); **The Boeing Company:** 52 (top right), 89 (bottom), 90 (top); **Experimental Aircraft Association:** 26, 30 (left); Jim Koepnick: 76; **Ford Motor Company:** 39 (center); **Foto Consortium:** Charles Mussi: 95 (right center); **Mike Hagel:** 28; **Kulik Photo/DOD/MGA:** 82 (top right); **Lockheed Aeronautical Systems Company:** 91, 96 (top center); **Lockheed Corporation:** 34; **McDonnell Douglas:** 40 (center), 82 (top left); Harry Gann: 38, 40 (top), 41 (top), 44 (bottom), 45 (bottom right); **National Air and Space Museum/Smithsonian Institution:** 9 (top), 12, 13, 14, 15, 16, 18 (center, bottom), 20, 23 (bottom), 25, 27, 30 (right), 31, 32, 35, 36, 37, 40 (bottom), 43 (top, bottom), 46-47, 48 (top left, top right), 49 (bottom), 59, 61, 63 (bottom), 65, 68 (top, center, bottom left), 69 (bottom), 73, 75 (top right, bottom left, bottom right), 77 (top), 78 (bottom right, bottom left), 79, 83 (bottom), 88; **Northrop/McDonnell Douglas:** 96 (bottom center); **Photri:** 5 (bottom right), 7, 18 (top), 21 (right), 45 (bottom left), 70 (top), 84 (center), 86, 87, 95 (top), 96 (bottom); **Steve Ritchie:** 85 (top); **United States Air Force:** 95 (left center, bottom); **United States Air Force Art Collection:** George Akimoto: 45 (top); Jay Ashurst: 11, 58-59; John Balsley: 69 (top); Merv Corning: 21 (left); James Diete: 53 (top left); Louis A. Drendel: 81; Keith Ferris: 5 (top), 6-7; Robert Horvath: 23 (top); Paul Jones: 66-67; Fritz Junghans: 65; John McCoy: 19; Stephen McElroy: 84 (top); Bill Phillips: 84 (bottom); Ahmed Ragheb: 85 (bottom); Rick Ruhman: 50-51; R.G. Smith: 42; William Yenne: 94; **United States Air Force Museum:** 4 (top), 70 (bottom); **United States Air Force Courtesy National Air and Space Museum/Smithsonian Institution:** 4 (center), 37 (top), 41, 43 (center), 44 (top), 48 (bottom left), 52 (top left, bottom), 53 (top right, bottom right), 54, 55, 56, 57, 59 (top), 60, 62, 63 (top), 68 (bottom), 71, 78 (top), 80; **United States Department of Defense:** 83 (top); **Wright State University Archives:** 8, 10.

Front Cover: National Air and Space Museum/Smithsonian Institution (top); Harley Copic/United States Air Force Art Collection (bottom left); Ford Motor Company (bottom right). **Back Cover:** United States Air Force Art Collection: Guy Deel (top); George Guzzi (center); Mark Waki (bottom).

Walter J. Boyne is a retired colonel in the United States Air Force and a prominent military consultant and writer. He has flown over 5,000 hours in many different aircraft, from a Piper Cub to a B-1B. Mr. Boyne is a former director of the National Air and Space Museum and is the best-selling author of *The Smithsonian Book of Flight, Weapons of Desert Storm,* and *Eagles At War,* the second novel of a projected trilogy.

Introduction

In making a list of classic aircraft, you can be sure of two problems. First, you will always make some people angry because the classic of their choice is not selected. Second, you will be torn by indecision as you evaluate the merits of the contenders. Yet the very inevitability of the first problem renders it inconsequential, while the second can be easily solved by making other lists, as many as you wish, for the history of aviation is rich with aircraft that deserve the honor.

The term "classic aircraft" can be defined narrowly, as in the hotly contested competitions conducted by the Experimental Aircraft Association at the annual Oshkosh Fly-In, where the thickness of chrome plating on a nut can determine the difference between winner or loser. Or the term can be defined broadly, to include just about any aircraft that has distinguished itself by its technical contribution, its service, its longevity, the esteem in which it is held, or simply by its appearance.

In this affectionate look at classic aircraft, the term will be interpreted broadly, so that a rich mixture of aircraft types can be selected. The rationale for selection will vary; some aircraft will *not* appear simply because they always appear in every listing made of classic aircraft. Others will surprise some readers by their relative obscurity. Still others will seem exactly appropriate.

The editors have attempted to achieve as broad a sampling as possible of classics, in terms of chronology, technology, and country of origin. The classics are arranged in chronological order, and the text for each aircraft is accompanied by striking photographs and art, many of them quite rare, and all visually informative. The goal in both text and illustration is to provide a fresh insight into the history of the aircraft, and to highlight the reasons why it is a classic. In truth, this is just a sampling of the possibilities, a connoisseur's sip from the heady cask of wine that is aviation history.

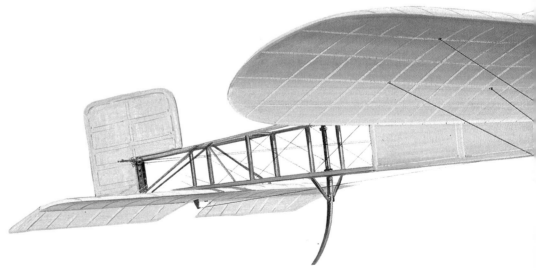

Left: This replica of a Sopwith Camel recreates one of history's greatest aircraft. The snub-nosed Camel was notorious for its quirky behavior, which was responsible for sending many inexperienced pilots to an early grave. But the Camel was a superior dogfighter, as evidenced by the 1,294 enemy planes Camel pilots downed in World War I.

Right: Mechanics perform maintenance on the engine of a C-47, the military version of the Douglas DC-3 commercial airliner. A product of the early 1930s, the design of the DC-3 was so fundamentally sound that today, nearly five decades after the first models were introduced, many of the aircraft remain in active service as passenger airliners and cargo carriers.

Above: The tiny, rickety-looking Bleriot XI became an instant classic when its creator, Louis Bleriot, used it to make the first flight across the English Channel in 1909.

Fortresses Engaged, by artist Keith Ferris, depicts a formation of Boeing B-17 Flying Fortresses being attacked by German Messerschmitt Bf-109 fighters. The B-17 was the staple aircraft of the U.S. daylight bombing campaign against Germany in World War II. Rugged, reliable, and beautiful, this much beloved plane remains a potent symbol of American air power in the struggle against the Axis.

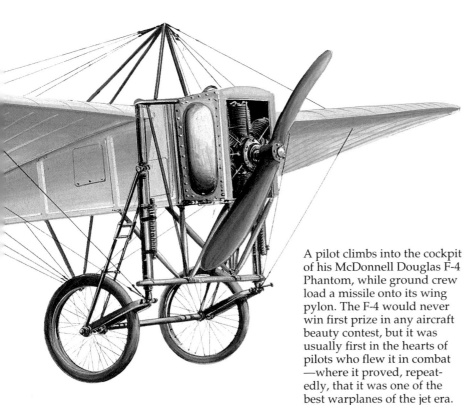

A pilot climbs into the cockpit of his McDonnell Douglas F-4 Phantom, while ground crew load a missile onto its wing pylon. The F-4 would never win first prize in any aircraft beauty contest, but it was usually first in the hearts of pilots who flew it in combat —where it proved, repeatedly, that it was one of the best warplanes of the jet era.

1905-1908 Wright Flyers

The first practical aircraft were also real hummers in flight

Main image, top: Orville Wright and Lt. Benjamin D. Foulis race above the crowd at Fort Myer in *The Dream Fulfilled - 30 July 1909*, by Keith Ferris. *Above*: An early Wright Flyer, as drawn by John Batchelor.

Almost every list of classic aircraft includes the original Wright Flyer that hangs so proudly in the exact center of the National Air and Space Museum. And with good reason, for the Kitty Hawk Flyer is undoubtedly *the* classic airplane of all time. It has accordingly been an oft-written about topic (in such books as Harry Combs' fine *Kill Devil Hill*, for example); and, to be sure, all of the attention it has received is well deserved. Forever overshadowed by its fame, however, are the Wright brothers' later aircraft, which are discussed here. These airplanes also contributed much to the growth of aviation. They are classics in their own right and, as such, are equally worthy of our attention.

History records that Orville and Wilbur Wright successfully undertook the first sustained, controlled flight by an aircraft operating under its own power at Kitty Hawk, North Carolina, on December 17, 1903.

Orville made the first and third flights; Wilbur the second and fourth. Many years were to pass before the true magnitude of their achievement was fully understood. Thus, despite what they had accomplished, fame and fortune initially eluded them. Due to press coverage that was both limited and wildly inaccurate, what should have been recognized as an epoch-making event was either ignored or greeted with outright disbelief—except by stock promoters who saw an opportunity to bilk both the Wrights and the public. This flutter of business activity was the harbinger of more than a decade of acrimonious business dealings that drained the Wrights of their initiative, and much of their charm.

In effect, modern aviation had taken wing under the Wrights' tutelage, and scarcely anyone had noticed. Curiously, this situation temporarily worked to the Wrights' advantage. The public was kept igno-

The camera freezes a golden moment for eternity as Orville Wright lifts from the sands at Kitty Hawk in the original Flyer. Note Wilbur running alongside the plane.

7

Wilbur and Orville with the 1904 Flyer II at Huffman Prairie, Ohio.

Above: The Wright biplane passes over the derrick catapult launcher system designed by the brothers to assist takeoff. *Right*: Wilbur Wright, characteristically sober-faced, grasps the controls of his Flyer. *Below*: Wilbur and a passenger fly over transportation of another era at Pau, France, where the Wrights established the world's first aviation school in 1909.

rant of the Flyer's many flaws, as well as the dangers involved in operating it—dangers so great as to raise legitimate concerns about the brothers' chances for a long life. Their hazards were implicit in the difficulties they overcame. First of all they had to refine much of the scientific data that had been pioneered by three innovators in the field of aviation: Samuel Langley, Otto Lilienthal, and Octave Chanute. They had to design and build their own engine and propeller combination, and they had to teach themselves to fly while designing the control mechanism of their gliders. When at last they flew their powered aircraft, it was inherently unstable, had a very narrow margin between stall speed and top speed, and was difficult to control. That they did not meet with tragedy early on is attributable to three main factors: the Flyer's extraordinarily oversensitive forward elevator (also known as a canard), which had an inherent tendency to prevent a stall; the careful preparation that typified all of their efforts; and, perhaps most important, an enormous measure of good luck.

Determined to improve on their aircraft, the Wrights spent 1904 developing a second Flyer, which they flew from Huffman Prairie, a field located 15 miles east of Dayton near a railroad stop called Simms Station. The new Flyer was almost identical in appearance to the original, but was slightly heavier, and had less wing curvature and a more powerful engine. It made its public debut during first trials on May 23, 1904. Media reaction varied from amusement to indignation when the second "Flyer" resolutely refused to fly.

This non-flight had occurred because the Wrights, clever as they were, had failed to take into account the effect of temperature and pressure altitude variations on their aircraft. At Kitty Hawk, a 34-degree temperature had resulted in an equivalent altitude of 1,800 feet below sea level. On Huffman Prairie, where the temperature had been 81 degrees, the equivalent altitude was 2,900 feet above sea level—a 4,700-foot differential that grounded the second Flyer securely to the prairie floor.

The Wrights overcame the problem by resorting to a crude expedient:

flinging their machine into the air with a catapult powered by a falling weight. Yet even with the added boost the catapult provided, it was not until their forty-ninth flight that they were able to match the 59-second duration of their first flight at Kitty Hawk. This occurred on September 15, 1904. In subsequent flights that same year, they completed the first circle in the air, and managed to remain airborne for as long as five minutes. Still, they had not yet built an aircraft that could be flown consistently from Point A to Point B.

That great achievement came in June of the next year. It was accomplished by the 1905 Wright Flyer III, which thereby earned a place in aviation history as the first practical airplane. The Flyer III had a span of 40 feet, six inches; it weighed 710 pounds, and employed the engine, propeller, and chains of the 1904 machine. As with the Kitty Hawk Flyer, the pilot lay prone on the lower wing of the Flyer III, operating the controls with a hip cradle. The two aircraft also had wing profiles that were curved in the same proportions. The Flyer III nevertheless represented a marked improvement over its illustrious predecessor. It was stronger; it possessed enhanced stability (accomplished by increasing the distance of the forward elevator from the wings); and it was driven by an engine capable of a sustained 25-horsepower output—more than twice the horsepower available to the original machine.

And Flyer III was a hummer, with the Wrights making over 40 flights in the aircraft from June to October. In the course of those five months the brothers were often to be found circling over the prairie, flying until their fuel was nearly depleted, sometimes chasing flocks of birds in a spirit of *joi de vivre,* and even registering the first bird strike when Wilbur collided with a starling.

On October 5, Wilbur flew for a distance of 24.2 miles, averaging a then-sensational 38 miles per hour! In doing so he stayed aloft for an unprecedented 39 minutes, 23 seconds, all spent in the prone position with his head raised. An exceptionally stiff neck the following day persuaded Wilbur and his brother to equip their next aircraft with an upright seating arrangement, despite

A Bitter Rivalry

The most bitter and counterproductive legal dispute in aviation history was waged by people who under any other circumstances would have become good friends. Their backgrounds were similar, their scientific and sporting interest the same, their talents complementary. Yet the ugly business of patent rights was to cast the Wright brothers and Glenn Curtiss into years of litigation, and effectively remove the joy from their aviation careers.

Curtiss was an inventor, a bicycle and motorcycle racer, and an entrepreneur. His skill in building light-weight, powerful motorcycle engines brought him to the attention of the famous Dr. Alexander Graham Bell, who invited him to join the Aerial Experiment Association (AEA), together with Doug McCurdy, Casey Baldwin, and the ill-fated Tom Selfridge (who was killed in the crash of the Wright Military Flyer). This happy little team experimented with propeller-powered boats, ice sleds, and airships. The association also corresponded with the Wrights, asking for information to build an aircraft. The Wright's replies were guarded but helpful, and on March 12, 1908, Casey Baldwin flew a biplane called the Red Wing from the frozen surface of Keuka Lake at Hammondsport, New York. The flight of 318 feet, 11 inches was widely hailed by the press as "the first public flight of an airplane in the United States."

The Wright brothers were not amused.

Glenn Curtiss (*middle*) with fellow AEA members.

The next year, the AEA scored further successes in two aircraft which used ailerons for lateral control, as did subsequent Curtiss aircraft. The Wrights considered this a clear infringement of their patents, and in August 1909 they filed suit against Curtiss to stop him from either exhibiting or selling airplanes.

This, the first of many legal actions for the Wrights, proved a fatal blow to their creativity. Consumed by court appearances, they devoted little time or energy to aviation. In 1912, Wilbur died of typhoid fever—the Wright family would always contend that Curtiss had driven him to the grave—and the great partnership of brotherly genius was ended.

But not the lawsuits. The issue remained unresolved until the First World War, when the government imposed a pooling of aircraft patents. The legal wrangling between Orville Wright and Glenn Curtiss ceased, but the personal enmity never ended. It cost the Wrights and Curtiss much, and aviation even more.

Wreckage of the 1908 Flyer in which Lt. Tom Selfridge lost his life.

While two German assistants turn the propellers, Orville (*right*) adjusts the engine of his plane at Berlin's Tempelhoff Field in 1909.

It is perhaps too much to expect that these two great aviation pioneers should also be good businessmen, and they were not. While the Wrights fumed over the obdurate stupidity and greed of the governments they were trying to help—for both men truly believed that the aircraft would contribute to the permanent elimination of armed conflict—foreign inventors were fast gaining on them. Although lacking in knowledge and experience, these foreigners were making great strides with a hell-for-leather approach to aircraft development that contradicted the Wrights' careful methods even as it traded on their success. Nevertheless, the Wright Flyers were still greatly superior to their European counterparts. By 1907, for example, the best aircraft in Europe, a Voison-Farman, had remained aloft for only one minute, under the most marginal control.

the additional drag this would entail.

Their aching necks notwithstanding, the Wrights had achieved considerable progress in the areas of aircraft speed, flight distance, and most especially, control. The Wrights had devised separate controls for pitch, roll, and yaw, thereby setting a definitive pattern for future aircraft designs. Ironically, this, the greatest of their many contributions, would involve them in years of painful litigation.

Upon completing Flyer III trials, the Wrights were understandably satisfied that they had mastered the intricacies of flight. Accordingly, they ceased flying for 30 months in order to concentrate on selling their invention to a disbelieving world. It was a frustrating process. The U.S. Army, displaying classic bureaucratic stu-

pidity, insisted that it could not fund the *development* of an aircraft; an assertion that seemed to indicate that those in a position to decide on such matters had taken leave of their collective senses, inasmuch as the Wrights were offering them an already fully developed aircraft.

Despairing, the brothers then tried, and failed, to strike a deal with Britain. Like the U.S. Army, the British balked at paying the Wrights' enormous asking price of $200,000— and this, for an aircraft the brothers wouldn't allow them to see until after a contract had been signed. As for the French, they had been most generous in applauding the Wrights; however, the French government could not bring itself to buy an aircraft that was not a product of France's (potential) aeronautical genius.

Prior to 1908, the Wrights had steadfastly refused to give public demonstrations of their aircraft—an attempt to keep would-be competitors from pirating their designs. This policy soon proved counterproductive, provoking hostility and criticism in the popular press and in scientific circles as well. Many people began to question the veracity of their claims as well as the authenticity of their deeds. This was particularly the case in France, where the Wrights were ridiculed as poseurs who would be properly bested by the host of French aircraft straining to leave the ground. Already Frenchman Henri Farman had made a circular flight of one kilometer, remaining airborne for nearly 90 seconds. Here, the French figured, was the man to put paid to the myth of the Wrights!

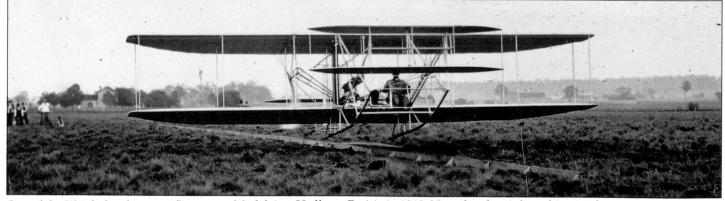

One of the Wright brothers test-flies a new Model A at Huffman Prairie in 1910. Note the plane's launching track.

The Wrights responded with a one-two punch that made aviation history. Returning briefly to Kill Devil Hill, the Wrights brushed up on their flying skills at the controls of the 1905 Flyer. Having regained their proficiency as pilots, the brothers temporarily parted ways, the better to sell their product. While Orville pursued a more reasonable contract with the U.S. Army, Wilbur embarked for France on a steamship. Arriving on the continent in May, Wilbur established himself at a facility in Le Mans, there to prepare his aircraft for flight. This he proceeded to do in his usual deliberate fashion, often sending to Dayton for various parts.

The resultant delays in the Flyer's public unveiling were regarded by the French with all manner of open discourtesy. Fellow aviators took a combative stance toward the elder Wright; by the same token, members of the press expressed their opinion of Wilbur and his aircraft in snidely derisive articles. Finally, on August 8, Wilbur produced his aircraft for a demonstration flight over the Le Mans racecourse. A decidedly hostile, if interested, crowd was on hand to witness the event. Spectator attitudes underwent an abrupt 180-degree change in Wilbur's favor once he got into the air. In a flight lasting one minute, 45 seconds, Wilbur steered the Flyer through a series of steep banks and skillful turns, describing two complete circles before returning to earth; and just like that, the Wrights became heroes of France. All the doubts about their aircraft, all the insults the Wrights had been forced to endure, had suddenly been dispelled by the Flyer's performance. Among the aviators present, jeers changed to cheers; and once Wilbur had set down, they crowded around his machine, determined, in the most professional and collegial way, to steal as many of his design secrets as possible.

Wilbur continued to dazzle Europe with aviation feats for the rest of the year, making more than 1,000 flights, setting records almost every day, winning prize after prize—and establishing the ground work for many potentially lucrative contracts.

In the United States, Orville achieved an equal measure of success. Sadly, though, it was marred by

Our Prices Like "Wilbur" Are Wright - BLDG 1402, by Jay Ashurst, depicts the Wrights' flying School in Montgomery, Alabama, 1910.

tragedy. The Army, now dimly aware that the Wrights were offering not an idea but a real airplane, had agreed to trials of a two-seat Flyer at Fort Myer, beginning on September 3, 1908. Like Wilbur, Orville was an audacious yet capable pilot; among the many aviation feats he performed during these trials was a flight lasting one hour, two minutes, and 15 seconds. On September 17, he flew, somewhat reluctantly, with Lieutenant Tom Selfridge (a member of the Aerial Experiment Association, rivals to the Wrights) in the passenger seat of the flyer.

The two men were making their fourth circuit of Fort Myer when disaster struck. At a height of about 100 feet, Orville heard a slight tapping in the rear of the machine. Orville saw nothing to indicate that they were in any danger, but for caution's sake he reduced power and began to descend. Suddenly two big thumps shook the Flyer, which then veered and dove straight down. In a subsequent letter to Wilbur, Orville wrote that "Lieutenant Selfridge up to this time had not uttered a word . . . But when the machine turned headfirst for the ground, he exclaimed 'Oh! Oh!' in an almost inaudible voice."

They crashed from a height of about 75 feet. Selfridge was killed, becoming the first person to die in a powered aircraft.

It was later determined that a crack in the right propeller was ultimately to blame for the crash. The crack had produced a slight deformation in the propeller, setting up a vibration that had caused the other propeller to sever a critical wire brace. Seconds before impact, Orville had nearly regained control of the aircraft after shutting off its engine. But he simply could not overcome the relentless chain of events that would typify future aviation accidents.

Despite the negative publicity engendered by this incident, the Wright idea in aircraft design soared in popularity as well as in fact. The later Wright Flyers were similar in appearance and dimension to the original, with major visual differences apparent in the twin seats on the leading edge, and in the proportions of the front and rear surfaces. The skies over Europe were soon crowded with dozens of these aircraft. At home, the Wrights' brilliant success would be diminished when fierce competition with Glenn Curtiss (see sidebar), among others, turned their attention from invention to litigation. Within a few years, Wright aircraft would no longer be competitive in the world market.

But for three glorious years, from 1905 to 1908, there was literally nothing in the world to compare with the classic Wright Flyers.

Bleriot XI

Serious design flaws did not prevent this homely little aircraft from conquering the European skies

In appearance the Bleriot XI was a singularly unprepossessing aircraft. A tiny monoplane originally powered by a clattering seven-cylinder REP engine, the XI had a nose that was too short, wings that were too long, and an open-trellis fuselage that offered too little protection for the pilot. Almost ignored when it first appeared, it went on to blaze a pioneering trail across the English Channel on July 25, 1909 (see sidebar), establishing both an unforgettable first and an aviation empire. Following the Channel flight, the Bleriot XI was produced in great numbers for both civilian and military purposes. The XI became a prolific record-setter, with aviators such as Roland Garros and George Chavez using it to make first flights across the Mediterranean and the Alps, respectively. Any one of these characteristics might merit the airplane being called a classic; to have them all is remarkable.

Sadly, the Bleriot XI had another, less appealing, claim to fame. Although the XI's design represented the peak of contemporary aviation design, it also contained a structural flaw that would cost the lives of many aviators, and cause the monoplane design concept to fall into disrepute for many years.

The Bleriot XI's namesake—short, swarthy, plucky Louis Bleriot—had little to do with actually designing the aircraft. The XI was instead the work of Raymond Saulnier, whose name became immortal with the famous series of Morane-Saulnier parasols in World War I and after. But Louis Bleriot provided the wherewithal for the aircraft, financing both the factory in which it was built, as well as the preceding series of aircraft from which it derived. In

Above: A precursor to the XI, this Bleriot VIII was powered by a 50 hp Antoinette engine with a four-blade propeller. *Main image, opposite:* Artist's rendering of the Bleriot XI near the White Cliffs of Dover, in the final minutes of Louis Bleriot's record-setting flight across the English Channel in 1909.

addition, some of his earlier ideas were incorporated in the XI's design.

The Bleriot XI debuted at the annual Paris automobile show in December 1908. It was one of three aircraft exhibited by the Bleriot firm, the other two being the Bleriot IX, a monoplane; and the Bleriot X, a biplane. None of the three aircraft had ever been flown, and the IX and X models, which were larger than the XI, would in fact never get off the ground. Nevertheless, the IX and X were, by virtue of their size, the star attractions of the show; the XI, with its diminutive 21-foot wingspan and puny 30-horsepower REP engine, was simply too small to generate much interest among the crowds thronging the exhibition hall. From a design standpoint, however, the XI was an impressive aircraft that boasted several advanced features: a monoplane wing mounted on pylon supports; a three-wheel landing gear complete with a complex shock-absorption system; and the Bleriot control system, which featured wing warping as its lateral control device.

The latter was an adaptation of the Wright wing warping system, which Bleriot had put to use without any thought whatsoever for paying the requisite license fee. It is interesting to note that Bleriot had previously been one of the most vocal critics of the Wright brothers; after Wilbur Wright's 1908 Le Mans flight, however, he became one of their greatest fans, as evidenced by the alacrity with which he appropriated their ideas. Wing warping would be one of the keys to the success of Bleriot's aircraft, which would shortly be pouring out his Paris factory at an astounding rate—a situation that must prompt sympathy for the hapless Wrights, who received not a penny in recompense.

Louis Bleriot flew the XI for the first time on January 23, 1909. He subsequently modified the aircraft by enlarging the wings and rudder, removing a central fin, and arranging the elevons (a device that combines the functions of elevators and ailerons) to perform solely as elevators. By May he had flown the aircraft often enough to become confident in its capabilities. He also found a new engine for it. The three-cylinder Anzani he installed was less powerful than the REP, delivering about 25 horsepower in an earsplitting, oil-spitting roar that left Bleriot deafened and greasy after every flight. But the Anzani was lighter than the REP, and it used a two-blade propeller, which was more efficient than the REP's four-blade propeller. Moreover, the Anzani could run for nearly an hour without quitting, as opposed to the majority of engines that were liable to overheat and give out after only a few minutes.

Like so many aircraft manufacturers, then and now, Bleriot was con-

Above: In its heyday, an exhibition flight by the Bleriot XI was a sure-fire crowd draw. In this photo, spectators have climbed atop their automobiles to witness an overflight by Louis Bleriot's marvelous monoplane.

Right: A Bleriot XI engages the rapt attention of four small children, who thus convey the sense of miracles coming to pass that early flights such as this one so often inspired.

A Bleriot XI's one-man ground crew keeps the plane pointed in the right direction during take-off. Presumably an agile fellow, he would have to jump aside at the last moment (before the plane became airborne) to avoid being clipped by the elevator.

stantly pressed for funds. As a manufacturer of acetylene headlamps and other automotive accessories—he was sort of an early Parisian Pep Boys—Bleriot had achieved wealth and fame. Without a second thought he had plunged into aviation, investing all of his savings and his wife's dowry—the better part of a million francs—into a long line of unsuccessful airplanes. Now, with the Bleriot XI, he at last had an aircraft with undeniable commercial possibilities. Aware that the marketability of a product hinges on public awareness, Bleriot entered a series of aircraft competitions in which the XI's qualities could be advertised to a wide audience. In the process he won a great deal of money and, not incidentally, suffered more than a few mishaps. None of these mishaps were fatal, but many were quite painful; during a 48-hour endurance flight, for instance, a malfunctioning exhaust pipe inflicted third-degree burns on his left foot. And he had walked, or at the very least hobbled, away from more than his share of crash landings. But any injuries thereby incurred were all in a day's work for Bleriot, who was willing to sacrifice much, including, evidently, his physical well-being, in order to boost aircraft sales.

As intended, Bleriot's flight across the English Channel virtually assured the commercial success of the XI. With purchase orders for the XI pouring in, the Bleriot firm rushed the aircraft into mass production while Bleriot himself continued his exhibition work. Ultimately over 800 XIs were built by Bleriot factories, and hundreds more were produced by other countries. Of the foreign models, some were turned out under license, while others were illegal copies, produced with the same high-handed disregard for paying license fees that Louis Bleriot had accorded the Wright brothers.

The burgeoning number of XIs required Bleriot to expand his operation, which meant building a new factory, laying out new airfields, and creating a pilot instructor corps. The whole business took on a wonderfully international flair, as foreign students and purchasing officers of foreign governments flocked to France, the former to receive pilot training

First Across the English Channel

In 1908, Lord Northcliffe, via his newspaper, the London *Daily Mail*, offered a prize of five hundred pounds for the first aircraft to make a non-stop flight across the English Channel between sunrise and sunset, either from England to France, or vice versa. The prospect of winning such a prize set a host of magnificent young men in motion, among them Louis Bleriot—who needed the money badly, but the acclaim even more.

To Lord Northcliffe's dismay, there were no English contenders. Instead, the quest for aviation's most coveted honor was undertaken by a pair of Frenchmen. One was the handsome, colorful Hubert Latham; the other was the volatile, mustachioed, plain-but-determined Louis Bleriot.

Latham's aircraft of choice was the beautiful Levavasseur Antoinette IV, a monoplane powered by an advanced 50 horsepower V-8 engine, and equipped with ailerons. It should also have been equipped with pontoons, for on July 15 Latham had covered only six miles from the French coast when his engine quit, forcing him down in the English Channel—where his rescuers found him perched on the sodden but buoyant wreckage of his aircraft, smoking a cigarette with Gallic aplomb.

Latham quickly procured a second Antoinette for another attempt. But this time, Bleriot beat him to the punch. The date was July 25, 1909. While Latham slept soundly in a Calais hotel, Bleriot had risen in the predawn darkness to begin preparing his aircraft, a Bleriot XI, for the flight to Dover. Already bothered by pain stemming from recent surgery on his foot, Bleriot's nerves were further strained when a stray dog ran into his whirling propeller and was chopped to bits. Nonetheless, he made a quick trial flight, and at 4:41 a.m., took off into the graying sky.

It took iron nerve to fly his fragile aircraft over the tossing waters of the Channel, and Bleriot was not found wanting in this regard. Without a compass to guide him, he pressed on toward the English coast with only the vaguest notion of where he would eventually set down. Some 20 minutes into his flight, he discerned the chalky line of Dover's cliffs looming before him. By then the Anzani engine that

Above: Hubert Latham's Antoinette IV takes off from the Calais beach, causing the horse of a French gendarme to shy away in panic. The hard-luck Latham was twice forced to ditch on two Channel attempts.

Left: Biting back fear and pain (his leg had been badly burned on a previous flight), a typically dour Louis Bleriot sits at the controls of his XI, only minutes before he embarked on his history-making journey across the English Channel. Bleriot was a fearless pilot who overcame numerous injuries in his quest for aviation fame.

powered his aircraft was dangerously overheated and losing power. It is probably a myth that a providential rain shower cooled the stuttering engine just as it was about to burn itself out; but it is not entirely unreasonable to conclude that providence, in one form or another, came to Louis Bleriot's assistance that day. Realizing that his plane was incapable of over-flying the Dover cliffs, Bleriot steered through an opening in the cliff wall and continued on to a rough field where, with enormous relief, he crash-landed in a style that had become almost customary with him. The elapsed time of his flight, from take-off to landing, was 36 minutes.

The dramatic impact his flight made upon the citizenry of both England and France was not duplicated until Charles Lindbergh soloed the Atlantic in 1927. Bleriot had become aviation's man of the hour, and deservedly so. He had flown across a hazardous body of water in an aircraft that had no instrumentation, a narrow margin between stall speed and top speed (22 and 45 miles per hour, respectively), and an agonizingly slow response to control inputs. The extent of Bleriot's triumph, so difficult to grasp in an age of supersonic jet travel, was fully comprehended by his fellow aviators, who now came to France in droves to buy his planes.

BLERIOT XI

The XI's open cockpit offered little shelter to pilots, who often did not wear seat belts or parachutes. Harriet Quimby (shown here) was one of many pilots to be killed in the Bleriot monoplane. In July 1912, while participating in the Harvard-Boston Aviation Meet, she fell to her death when her plane flipped upside down in mid-flight.

Rescuers pull a mortally injured George Chavez from his wrecked Bleriot XI, which crashed on September 23, 1910.

(free if you purchased a Bleriot aircraft, $150.00 if you did not), the latter to acquire Bleriot XIs for their respective armed forces.

While all this was going on, Louis Bleriot found that exhibition flying and, indeed, the Bleriot XI itself, had become rather old hat. Seeking a fresh challenge, he began developing new aircraft designs, none of which were to have the impact of the Bleriot XI. The failure of the new designs was due in part to Bleriot's policy of continuously modifying and improving the design of the XI, and adapting it to special needs. Trainers were sorely needed by fledgling pilots and air forces alike, and the Bleriot factory provided them virtually on demand for about $2,500. For aerobatic pilots, special harnesses were devised to restrain the pilot when they performed such heretofore impossible stunts as loops and inverted flight. Sporting pilots could chose from a variety of one- and two-seat

types, some lavishly equipped with instrumentation. The military services of France, England, Rumania, Bulgaria, Turkey, Russia, Italy, and other countries all required, and obtained, highly customized versions of the XI.

Many of the modifications made to the Bleriot XI, while improving performance, also made the aircraft more dangerous to fly. This was especially true of the many Bleriot XIs used for racing—an endeavor that put aircraft strength to a severe test, even in an era of relatively slow speeds. More power, hence a faster aircraft, was readily available in the new series of Gnome rotary engines that had appeared on the scene. With modifications, the Bleriot XI airframe could accept Gnome rotaries ranging from 50 to 140 horsepower. Pilots might further augment engine horsepower by "tweaking" their aircraft—making custom improvements in the hope of gaining a few extra miles per hour. None of these alterations were engineered—they were all intuitive attempts to increase speed at any price, and ranged from flattening the curve of the airfoil to shortening the wingspan.

If raising horsepower raised speed, it also increased the strain on the airframe. In due course, this strain was made manifest in a series of crashes with a haunting pattern of similarity. The Bleriot's wings would fail, bending sharply as the spars snapped, thus causing the aircraft to plunge to the ground. Some of the great flyers of the day, undoubted masters of their machines, lost their lives in

seemingly inexplicable circumstances. The renowned Leon Delagrange died in the crash of a Bleriot XI in January 1910. The American Harriet Quimby, who became the first woman to fly across the English Channel on April 21, 1912, perished less than three months later when she fell from her aircraft; in both instances, she had been at the controls of a Bleriot XI. The list of aviators who met their demise in Bleriots also included such famous names as Hubert Leblon, George Chavez, and John Moisant. Soon grave doubts began to be voiced about monoplanes in general and the Bleriot XI in particular.

Louis Bleriot was aghast at these developments. After all, he had thoroughly tested all of his machines by the traditional method of piling sand bags on the wing until they collapsed. Judging by the results of such tests, he had thought that his airplane could sustain all the forces that acted upon it.

Unfortunately, his tests explored only certain areas of strength—and not the particular area of weakness. Bleriot responded in the only way he knew how, with a series of modifications to increase the strength of the wing spars and bracing wires. It was a brute-strength approach that proved ultimately effective only because the basic design itself was so limited in performance. It was not until well after the First World War had gotten underway that the Bleriot wing design was seen to be vulnerable to compression loads encountered in flight—loads which the sandbagging tests did not induce.

The Bleriot XI was comparatively obsolete by 1913. Nevertheless, it was actively engaged during the early months of World War I, and soldiered on well after that date in a training role, particularly as "penguins"—clipped-wing aircraft which, being unflyable, were used as a sort of primitive flight simulator.

Today the Bleriot XI's classic status is affirmed by the more than two dozen original versions of this aircraft that survive, along with a similar number of reproductions, in museums around the world. A very few are still flying, on calm mornings, when the air is strong—and the pilots are brave.

Sopwith Camel

The "fierce little rasper" was a notorious killer of enemy planes—and sometimes, friendly pilots

A pair of RFC Sopwith Camels patrol
the Western Front in this
John Batchelor painting.

SOPWITH CAMEL

The Sopwith Camel was an aircraft of complex traits, a mix of the temperamental and the brilliant that could leave men grasping for metaphors in their attempts to describe it. In one such attempt, then-Captain Norman McMillan of the Royal Flying Corps remarked that the Camel was "a buzzing hornet, a wild thing, burning the air like raw spirit fires the throat." And not only that; it was, he went on to say, "a fierce little rasper."

McMillan had meant to praise the Camel. Many pilots would agree with his assessment; some pilots, however, would not share his admiring sentiments. Understandably so, for the very qualities that made the Camel a dogfighter par excellence rendered it extremely difficult for inexperienced pilots to fly. The pilots who survived to master the Camel loved it; unfortunately, many young men—most under 20 years of age—were spun to their deaths by the quirky flying characteristics imparted by its short length and rotary engine. Yet there is no denying its ultimate status as a classic—the Sopwith Camel was the most successful Allied fighter, shooting down some 1,294 enemy aircraft.

Like its lineal descendant, the Hawker Hurricane, the Sopwith Camel was the right plane at the right time in history. Prior to its appearance, the Germans had introduced the elegant Albatros D I in September 1916, placing it in the hands of *Jagdstaffel* (fighter squadron) 2 under the command of the inimitable Captain Oswald Boelcke. With a high speed of 110 miles per hour and powerful twin machine gun armament, the Albatros dominated the skies. The rapidly expanded Albatros *Jastas* (an abbreviation of *Jadgstaffel*) decimated their Allied opponents in numerous aerial engagements, culminating in the murderous, one-sided fighting of Bloody April, 1917. Amidst this carnage, the most successful of the Albatros' opponents were built by Sopwith—the delightful Pup and the more formidable Triplane.

Although both were a pleasure to fly, the Pup and Triplane were somewhat fragile and underarmed, being equipped with only one machine gun. The two fighters were also too

The Camel's design was derivative of the much-loved Sopwith Pup (*top*), shown here in replica. *Above:* The Sopwith Triplane, or "Tripe," was used by the Royal Naval Air Service. Like the Pup, it was a delight to fly; and, like the Pup, it was fragile and undergunned.

stable for their own good, as well as the good of their pilots. In aircraft design, stability tends to cancel out maneuverability; hence the Pup and the Triplane, although docile and responsive to the pilot's touch, nevertheless lacked the aggressive agility needed to wrest air superiority from the German fighters.

At Sopwith's Kingston plant, four brilliant men pooled their talents to concoct an Albatros antidote. Of the four, the most prominent figure was none other than T.O.M. Sopwith himself, the founder of the firm and one of the truly great gentlemen of aviation. Sopwith directed the activities of a wonderfully inspired but utterly pragmatic team that consisted of Harry Hawker, a famous test pilot with a penchant for design; Fred Sigrist, a designer and a marvelous production manager; and Herbert Smith, the chief designer. Following company practice, they laid a blank sheet of paper over the general arrangement drawing of the Pup and, while retaining as much as was practical from that machine, they drew up plans for a new airplane that could significantly out-perform anything then flying.

The result of their efforts, the Sopwith F.1, was completed six weeks later in December 1916. The aircraft had the same conventional construction as its predecessors, but none of their aesthetic qualities. Snub-nosed and short-tailed, it gave the initial impression of a Pup that had been flown into a wall. But as if to prove that looks can be deceiving, the F.1's oddly blunted appearance signaled an aircraft possessed of extraordinary maneuverability. This was attained in part by moving the cockpit, fuel tank, and machine guns forward as close as possible to the engine, which served to concentrate

In profile, the Camel was said to resemble a Sopwith Pup that had been flown at top speed into a wall. The foreshortened fuselage concentrated the center of gravity forward, resulting in a more maneuverable, if unstable, aircraft.

maximum weight at the center of gravity; and by shortening the aft portion of the fuselage by eight inches, thereby reducing the overall length to 18 feet, nine inches. The aircraft was further distinguished by a 28-foot top wing that was made flat, at Sigrist's behest, to facilitate mass production. To compensate for the resultant loss in stability, the lower wings were given an exaggerated dihedral—the angle at which the wings are joined to the fuselage.

The F.1's most important attribute, at least from the standpoint of hard-pressed British fighter pilots, were the two synchronized Vickers machine guns mounted side-by-side in front of the cockpit. Here was an armament that could, at long last, match the firepower of the dreaded Albatros. Not only did the guns enable the British to fight on equal terms with German aircraft, they were also responsible for the unofficial, but ubiquitously used appellation by which the F.1 came to be known. Inspired by the humped fairing that encased the breeches of the two guns, Royal Flying Corps pilots, who customarily thought up nicknames for their aircraft, dubbed Sopwith's new fighter the "Camel."

To achieve more maneuverability than either the Pup or the Triplane possessed, the Sopwith team had deliberately designed the Camel to be unstable. Many a pilot trainee, his nerves badly shaken by an encounter with an uncontrollably spinning Camel, would agree that Sopwith and company had succeeded beyond their wildest dreams—and his nightmares. Powered by rotary engines (initially Clergets and Le Rhones, later by Bentleys), the lightweight Camels (only 1,470 pounds loaded) were notoriously susceptible to the effect of torque.

To understand what this means, one must comprehend how a rotary engine works. In such engines, the propeller is attached by a plate to the cylinders, which then turn as a combined unit around a stationery crankshaft. This novel solution to the cooling problem provided a powerful, lightweight engine with relatively low vibration. Within its whirling mass, however, there lurked a countervailing tendency to rotate the airframe in the opposite direction. This

Dog Fight, Cambrai, France, September 22, 1918, by John T. McCoy, Jr. McCoy's painting depicts RFC Camels engaging enemy Fokker D VIIs just 19 days before the war came to an end.

tendency can be reproduced on a much smaller scale with the kind of rubber band-powered model airplane available in most hobby shops. Simply wind up the rubber band, hold the propeller, and release the model. The airplane will rotate, thus demonstrating in part the principle of torque.

The engine torque meant that there would be no such thing as "hands off" flying in a Camel; rudder pressure had to be maintained constantly, varying with the speed and power, but maintained firmly nonetheless. Should a pilot remove his feet from the rudder bars, the Camel would skitter into a flat turn, and thence to a spin. At full throttle, the aircraft was extremely tail-heavy, forcing the pilot to press forward constantly on the stick—a laborious process that led to difficulties in aiming and shooting the guns during a dogfight. If a wounded pilot's hand slipped from the stick, the Camel's nose would bound wildly upwards, carrying the aircraft to the edge of a stall and beyond.

There were other complications. In a right-hand turn, the Camel dropped its nose; turning to the left, the nose went up. Both tendencies had to be overcome by application of the

rudder. But the Camel was sensitive, and a kiss too much rudder in the turn could send it spinning toward the ground. There were, of course, no trim tabs to ease the pilot's burdensome efforts to control his aircraft. Consequently, aerial combat in a Camel could exhaust a pilot with the constant alteration of pressures as speeds increased and decreased. Flying the Camel was thus a twofold chore: even as the pilot was trying to hold to the desired course, he was struggling to keep his machine from zooming off in random directions.

When powered by the Clerget engine, as most of the early Camels were, the aircraft had a not entirely deserved reputation for killing student pilots. This cranky little 130-horsepower rotary engine required that a fine adjustment be made to lean the fuel mixture almost immediately after take-off, just as the Camel reached an altitude of about 200 feet. A student pilot, frantically working his head, hands, and feet to herd his fractious mount through its takeoff, would suddenly be forced to contend with a coughing Clerget. If he didn't react instantly to lean the mixture, the engine would die, and the tail-heavy Camel would snap its nose up into a stall and ruthlessly spin in.

Sir Thomas Sopwith

The founder of Sopwith Aircraft, Ltd., Sir Thomas Octave Murdoch Sopwith, died on January 27, 1989, at the age of 101; he was a man who was born blessed, created mightily, and lived well and fully. In his lifetime of achievement, Sopwith's quiet, decisive manner won him thousands of friends and a reputation for fair and honest dealing in both business and in the sports in which he was so passionately involved.

His father was wealthy, and provided him with an independent income, but not for Tom Sopwith was the life of the idle rich. A mechanically inclined lad, he found his true calling in 1910, when he witnessed the flight of a Bleriot aircraft while yachting at Dover. He was then 21 years old. Shortly thereafter the young Sopwith had purchased his own aircraft and taught himself to fly. He became a daring and skilled aviator, and was soon touring with an exhibition flying team in Europe and the United States. But flying was not enough—he next embarked upon a career in aeronautical design, one that would bring him world fame, establish two highly successful companies, and create aircraft that would play a significant role in two world wars.

Sopwith was a man of many talents and many interests who excelled at flying, sailing, motoring, and speed-boat racing. His greatest talent, though, may have been finding co-workers who complemented his own abilities. Fred Sigrist and Harry G. Hawker were two such men. Sopwith hired Sigrist, a former sailing crony, to build aircraft to his specifications; Hawker, a young Australian pilot, would test and demonstrate the completed products. The two men joined Sopwith in 1912 upon the formation of the Sopwith Aircraft Company, which was originally located in a converted skating rink in Kingston.

Sopwith's timing, as always, was impeccable. He had set up shop at a time of burgeoning public interest in aviation. In its first few years of operation, the Sopwith factory was constantly busy, turning out seaplanes, flying boats, and, most especially, the Sopwith Tabloid, a tiny biplane that was the true sire of the wartime fighters that were soon to follow. On floats, and powered by a 100-horsepower Gnome Monosoupape rotary, the Tabloid won the 1914 Schneider

Tom Sopwith, aviator.

Trophy with a top speed of 85 miles per hour; it then went on to establish a world's speed record of 92 miles per hour.

At the outbreak of the First World War in August 1914, the Sopwith firm was ready and able to manufacture warplanes. Among the great Sopwith aircraft that saw action in the war were the Sopwith 1-1/2 Strutter, Pup, Triplane, Camel, Dolphin, and Snipe. Of these, the Camel was unquestionably the most successful, although it should not be forgotten that the Pup and the Triplane were both excellent aircraft, while the Snipe, which saw only limited service toward the war's end, may have been the best of the Sopwith designs.

After the war the bottom dropped out of the aircraft industry, resulting in contract cancellations that compelled Sopwith to dissolve his firm. In its stead he created a smaller firm, the H.G. Hawker Engineering Company, Ltd. Demonstrating once again his talent for attracting extraordinarily capable men to work for him, Sopwith hired the brilliant Sidney Camm to be his chief designer. Camm's designs included the Fury, Hart, Hurricane, Typhoon, and Tempest. The latter three aircraft performed with distinction in World War II, achieving combat service records that elevated Hawker to the same level of renown attained by the Sopwith company in World War I. After the war the company changed its name to Hawker Siddeley, which produced the most popular of all British jet fighters, the Hunter.

Knighted in 1953, Sir Thomas Sopwith retired from the Hawker Siddeley Group in 1968. The esteem and affection accorded him by his countrymen would, in the final years of his long and productive life, be matched only by the affection and esteem aviation enthusiasts everywhere continue to feel for his magnificent aircraft.

Accidents of this sort occurred often—but not so often as later accounts would have it.

Adding insult to the prospect of injury and death was the Camel's penchant for spewing castor oil (which was used as an engine coolant) from its valves. While not a lethal flaw in the aircraft's design, this could lead to some rather undignified not to mention embarassing moments; as when Camel pilots, having gulped massive doses of castor oil mist sprayed back on them during flight, were stricken with a compelling need to relieve themselves upon returning to base.

Notwithstanding all the aforementioned drawbacks, the Camel came as a godsend to the embattled Royal Flying Corps. Veteran British pilots, accustomed to flying inferior aircraft, were quite taken with the new fighter. Air Vice Marshall Arthur Gould Lee, a former Pup pilot who had, despite the odds, engaged the fearsome Albatros every day in battle, was delighted to find that the Camel was roomier, had more power, and was even lighter on the controls than a Pup. The Pup, he noted, "is a gentle-sensitive, while the Camel is *fierce, razor sharp.*"

The aircraft's combat debut came on July 4, 1917, when five brand new Camels, their dark green, almost chocolate-colored fabric as yet unmarred by bullets holes and castor oil stains, darted up from their base at Dunkirk to battle 16 Gotha bombers returning from a daylight raid on London. According to some reports, two Gothas were brought down; if so it was a highly auspicious beginning for the Sopwith fighters.

The bombers were relatively easy pickings for the Camels. The real test would come in combat against German fighters. The Camels were more than up to the task. The Camel soon demonstrated it could turn quicker than any German fighter, and this was more than life insurance for Allied pilots; it was a license to kill. An experienced pilot could pull up the Camel's nose, cut the throttle, and make an almost instantaneous stall-turn, flicking around like a weather vane, disappearing from the enemy plane's gunsight to reappear on its tail. The Camel became the Albatros' death warrant.

The Camel performed well at low altitudes, and was effective at the 12,000-foot level. Much above this height, performance fell off rapidly. The plane was initially used in LOPs and DOPs—line offensive patrols and deep offensive patrols behind enemy lines. Four little 25-pound Cooper bombs could be slung on external racks below the fuselage (severely degrading the aircraft's performance), and Camels thus armed were used in attacks on railroad depots and enemy airfields.

Early on in their deployment, the Camels were also pressed into what many regarded as the most exciting and dangerous work of all, trench strafing and bombing. Taking off at dawn, bomb-laden Camels in line formation would descend on the enemy trenchworks, roaring down at perilously low altitudes where the near-constant bombardment of Allied and German artillery batteries filled the air with shells capable of obliterating an airplane—and its pilot—in an instant. Pilots often saw the huge projectiles streaking across their line of flight, creating a gust of air turbulence that rocked their frail stick-and-wire aircraft like wood chips on a storm-tossed sea. Ignoring these distractions, the Camel pilots dove on the German positions, machine guns chattering all the way down amid a hail of machine gun and rifle bullets fired from a thousand and more unseen sources on the ground. Strafing attacks were effective but costly; during the March 1918 battle of Cambrai, for instance, the low-level work caused a 30-percent loss rate among the Camel squadrons.

Given the casualties they suffered, it comes as no surprise to learn that Camel pilots employed in the ground attack role usually welcomed a return to air combat. In a dogfight with another plane their mounts were nimble enough to battle a known and visible enemy; better still, they were no longer targets for the random, and inglorious, hit from the ground.

Camels were involved in many classic aerial engagements. But the one destined to capture the world's imagination occurred on the morning of April 21, 1918. The sky was overcast that day, but not enough to deter the flight of a German fighter

Above: The Killer Camel, by Merv Corning, depicts the climactic moment of the dogfight that claimed the life of Manfred von Richthofen—the "Red Baron." *Inset:* The aristocratic Richthofen shot down 80 Allied aircraft by dint of his superb marksmanship.

squadron commanded by Rittmeister Manfred, Freiherr von Richthofen. Taking off in a welter of snarling engines, the 22 Fokker triplanes and Albatros D Vs of Richthofen's so-called "flying circus" formed up and headed for the front lines, intending to conduct a combat sweep just behind the Allied front lines.

With 80 victories to his credit, Richthofen had by this time virtually cemented his reputation as the supreme fighter ace of the First World War. As usual he was at the controls of a Fokker Dr I triplane, an aircraft he had been flying since September of the previous year, and which was painted in a deep-red color scheme—hence his nickname, the "Red Baron." Designed by Anthony Fokker as a counter to the Sopwith Triplane, the Dr I was smaller and slower than the Camel, but a shade more maneuverable. It also had a faster climb rate, which made it perfectly suited for Richthofen, the master hunter.

Since Richthofen's two most recent kills had been Camels, he was in no way daunted by the prospect of another encounter with the Sopwith fighters. And encounter them he did, over Sailly-le-Sec, when his circus pounced on a pair of British observation planes. The latter were escorted by a flight of Sopwith Camels, which promptly swarmed to their defense. The Camels were commanded by a Canadian, Captain Roy Brown, himself an ace with 11 victories. Flying with Brown was Lieutenant W. R. "Wop" May, a combat novice who, per preflight instructions, broke away from the ensuing action when his guns jammed. In doing so he became prey for Richthofen himself, who came hurtling down from altitude to attack the British pilot.

Accounts differ as to precisely what happened next. We know that Brown dropped down behind Richthofen, who was oblivious to the threat to his rear, so fixated was he on shooting at the Camel in front of

21

Of Beagles and Blipping: The Sopwith Camel In Popular Memory

It is ironic the Sopwith Camel is better known to more people now than it was in its First World War heyday. That this is so is due in large part to a lovable beagle named Snoopy, the popular character in Charles Schulz's "Peanuts" comic strip. As drawn by Schulz, Snoopy is an imaginative canine given to taking near-literal flights of fancy while seated atop his doghouse—which his fertile mind transforms into a Sopwith Camel. Wearing a leather flying helmet and goggles, he further imagines himself engaged in a series of humorous (and frustratingly inconclusive) aerial duels with the Red Baron, Manfred von Richthofen.

Introduced originally as just another of Snoopy's antics, the Camel/Red Baron motif has recurred over the years, reinforcing itself in the public's consciousness through the production of Snoopy dolls, U-control gas model airplanes, and various other toys and gimcracks too numerous to mention. The motif has also been employed quite properly in theme park settings, but less properly in museum aviation exhibits. Less properly, because a museum is really not the place for it. Museums are normally the venue of historical fact, and the facts concerning the Camel were often cruel. The fuzzy-warm glow emanating from Charles Schulz's undeniably delightful comic strip tends to soften the image of an aircraft that could be quite harsh to friend and foe alike.

But this would not be the first time that the Camel has been misrepresented. In Hollywood films, the Camel was often depicted with little more authenticity than Snoopy's bullet-riddled doghouse. Usually, the supposed Camels were actually Thomas Morse Scouts or Travel Air biplanes fitted out with ring cowls and machine guns.

Curiously, filmmakers used the Camel's rotary engine sound even while eschewing the plane itself. The Camel's throttleless Gnome Monosoupape (single valve) engine employed a multi-position ignition switch; on landing, power was adjusted by "blipping" the engine, essentially cutting power by cutting spark-plugs. Hollywood audio technicians loved the sound, and commonly dubbed it in on their soundtracks, so that pseudo-Camels were always psuedo-blipping, no matter what their flight regime.

It is in literature where the Camel assumes its rightful, and accurate, place in both the history and the mythology of aviation. Norman McMillan wrote evocatively of the Sopwith fighter in his memoir *Into the Blue*, as did Arthur Lee Gould in *No Parachute* and *Open Cockpit*. In *War Birds*, the irrepressible Elliot White Springs used a thinly fictionalized version of American pilot John McGavock Grider's diary, as well as his own experiences, to convey something of the joy and sorrow involved in flying Camels. There have also been numerous documentary histories, ranging from *Profile No. 31* to Jack Bruce's coverage in his inimitable *British Aeroplanes, 1914-1918*.

But to get a sense for how the Camel flew, and how Camel pilots felt about the plane, the single best source is *Winged Victory*, a novel by V. M. Yeates, himself a former Camel pilot. Beautifully written, packed with drama, *Winged Victory* presents what is unquestionably the truest, most honest picture of air combat in a Sopwith Camel.

Novice pilots, finding the Camel a difficult plane to master, often lost their lives in accidents like the one shown here.

Vaughn and Burdick, by Robert Horvath, shows the two RFC Camel pilots named in the title attacking a pair of German observation planes.

There were plenty of men to share in this feeling, as the Camel was now widely employed in every major theater of the war. In addition to service in the Royal Flying Corps and the Royal Naval Air Service, Camels were flown by the air arms of the United States, Belgium, Italy, Russia, and Greece. The Camels fulfilled a variety of roles, including that of air superiority fighter, ground support fighter, and night fighter. Moreover, ship-borne Camels were used to combat intruding Zeppelins, and bomb Zeppelin sheds; while experimental variants were developed for use as dive bombers, and to be dropped from dirigibles.

Some 5,094 Camels were eventually built. Following the armistice on November 11, 1918, Camels saw further combat in the Russian Civil War, when they were employed against Bolshevik forces by the Slavo-British Aviation Group. Also in the post-war period the Americans, who had flown Camels with great success during the war, conducted experiments in which the Sopwith fighters were flown from specially rigged turrets on the battleships *Texas* and *Arkansas*.

Some 5,094 Camels were built. In the final months of the war, newer aircraft would begin to supplant the Camel; none, however, would surpass the Camel in renown or achievement. To this day, Tom Sopwith's fierce little rasper stands forth as the quintessential fighter aircraft of World War I.

him. The three planes had swooped down to within a few feet of the ground when Brown commenced firing. Almost simultaneously, Australian machine gunners in the trenches below opened fire as well. The red triplane nosed up, then crash-landed in a field. Richthofen sat dead at his controls, shot through the chest by a .303 bullet.

Who killed the Red Baron? The answer to that question is still a matter of conjecture—and not a little controversy. Whether Brown or the Australians fired the death-dealing shot—both parties have their proponents—is impossible to determine; what is certain is that Richthofen had played a key role in his own demise. As disciplined as he was daring, Richthofen was known as the kind of pilot who simply didn't make mistakes. He normally selected his victims and executed his attacks with equal care. But not on this occasion. It is said that Richthofen was still suffering the ill-effects of a bullet wound to the head, sustained in combat the previous summer; and that the resultant headaches, aggravated by frayed nerves, had precipitated a marked deterioration in his skill and daring as a pilot. Physically exhausted and emotionally spent by the rigors of his

trade, the war-weary German ace had gotten careless. And in his carelessness, he had erred fatally by pursuing Lieutenant May across enemy lines, and by flying too low for too long on the tail of May's aircraft.

Despite claims to the contrary by Australian army troops, Allied airmen naturally assumed that the Red Baron had been downed by a Camel pilot. The morale of Camel pilots everywhere surged accordingly.

A Camel takes off from a British ship rigged for aircraft operations. Note the unusual feature of a wing-mounted machine gun.

Gotha G Series

Germany's big bombers ushered in a terrible new phase of warfare

Some aircraft are such inherent classics that they come to characterize their type—to many, all light planes are Cubs, all jet transports are 727s, all Soviet fighters are MiGs. In the First World War, one German plane became so famous that its name became a generic term for enemy bombers—the Gotha.

This boxy biplane, so similar to others of its type, owed much of its infamy to the indignant tone adopted by the media in reporting its combat debut over England. This tone struck a responsive chord in British citizens, who were quite taken aback by the spectacle of their heretofore unassailable island being subjected to attack by formations of Gothas operating with impunity above the reach of antiaircraft gunnery and fighter aircraft. And if the sight of Gothas calmly "circling and pirouetting overhead" wasn't sufficient to provoke outrage, there was the knowledge that the German aircraft were inflicting damage to private property and killing and injuring civilians. From the British standpoint, such actions were not only cruel but, equally as

objectionable, they were unsporting as well! To defend England from the Gothas, fighter aircraft had to be transferred from the Western Front, which had the effect of reducing air strength in a theater where it was sorely needed—which of course was precisely what the Germans had intended when they conceived the Gotha raids.

The Gotha was not the first bomber to attack civilian targets. The Austrians had used balloons to drop bombs on Venice in 1849, and the French had bombed civilian targets—reportedly villages, mosques, and flocks of sheep—in Morocco in 1912. The world was shocked in 1914 when more than 50 small bombs were dropped on Paris in raids by what became known as "the five-o'-clock Taube". On one occasion, the Taube pilot had the effrontery to drop a message informing the French populace that "The German Army is at the gates of Paris. You have no choice but to surrender. Lieutenant von Hindelsen." The Taube raids prompted American President Woodrow Wilson to write Germany's Kaiser

Wilhelm a stern letter of protest; somewhat more consequentially, the French registered their displeasure by bombing Freiburg. As is so often the case in war, one action begets another, similar reaction, producing what is now termed the "domino effect." So it was that, after the French retaliation, the dominos began falling in ernest, with the Kaiser authorizing Zeppelin raids against England—but not against London. When, later in the year, Karlsruhe was bombed by the Allies, the Kaiser included London in the list of permissible targets.

Thus, the Germans, although not the first to bomb civilian targets, introduced the concept of systematic attacks against targets where civilian casualties were inevitable. The Zeppelin raids began in 1915 and lasted through 1918. Zeppelins possessed two important advantages over contemporary bomber aircraft: they could fly great distances, and carry a large bombload.

A true measure of the impact of the Gotha is not possible without assessing the enormous scale of the Ger-

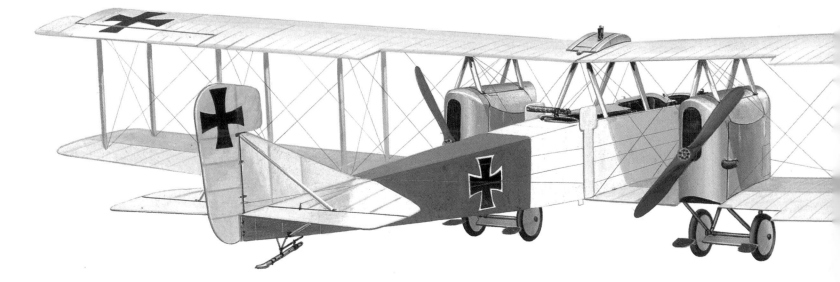

man Zeppelin effort. The image of the Zeppelin is now fixed for most of the world in the newsreels of the last moments of the burning Hindenburg, when the hazards of hydrogen-filled dirigibles were captured so graphically. The German Zeppelins of World War I were indeed hazardous—but they were also technological marvels, as long as an ocean liner, and capable of extraordinary feats. One of the later Zeppelins, the LZ 113, operating out of Nordholz, was 743 feet long, weighed 62,900 pounds empty, had a useful load of 112,700 pounds, was powered by six 240 horsepower Maybach engines, and had a top speed of 73 mph.

The Zeppelins flew almost 1,500 sorties, 306 of them against England, where in 51 raids they dropped slightly less than 200 tons of bombs. A total of 557 people were killed and 1,358 injured in the raids. Only about 50 crews were trained to fly the giant airships, and the cost to them was great—almost 40 percent were killed.

In addition to high casualties, there were other factors that mitigated against the use of Zeppelins. The hydrogen that bore them aloft was one. The gas, which was highly flammable, was a source of deep disquiet for Zeppelin crews; although accidents were minimized through discipline and training, crews could never quite escape the fear of immolation that a single errant spark might cause. Moreover, launching the air ships from their protective sheds was a tricky proposition; and a mission could only proceed during the new moon phase (when the absence of moonlight made them harder to spot), and when weather and wind conditions were favorable (storms could break the airships apart, or drive them so far off course that they could not return to base). Finally, their size and speed made them vulnerable to the rapidly building British air defense system. Tangible evidence of the system's effectiveness was provided with mounting frequency in the night sky over London, which was set brilliantly aglow when Zeppelins, hit by antiaircraft fire, plummeted downward in a nimbus of burning hydrogen. Later in the war, specially designed "height

A British soldier dry-fires the nose gun of a captured Gotha G Vb. This model is distinguished by the installation of two wheels beneath the nose.

British civilians inspect a Gotha shot down over England. Gothas, like the Zeppelins before them, shattered Britain's sense of security against direct attack.

A Gotha G V is readied for another mission against England. The psychological impact of Gotha attacks far outweighed the material damage they inflicted.

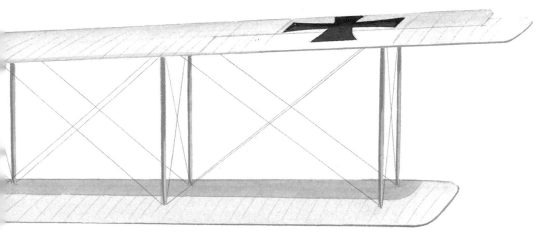

Rear view of a Gotha G IV, as conceived by artist John Batchelor. The Gotha had a relatively high performance for the time, being able to arrive over England at about 15,000 feet, which was initially beyond the capability of defending fighters.

climbers" could reach 20,000 feet, well beyond the reach of British fighters, but the cold and lack of oxygen were more trouble to Zeppelin crews than the Zeppelins were to the British.

The Gotha series of bombers offered a solution to the bombing problem. The first in the series was the G II. Introduced in 1916, this aircraft was an angular biplane powered by two straight-eight Mercedes pusher propeller engines, each capable of generating 220 horsepower. The main Gotha production types were the G IV and G V, which appeared in 1917. While externally similar to the G II, the later models featured the more powerful 260 horsepower Mercedes engines, which enabled it to operate at about 15,000 feet—the extreme limit of contemporary English air defenses.

All variants of the Gotha had a 77-foot upper wing span and a gross weight of 7,000 pounds—a huge airplane for its day. To get an idea of its size, consider that the World War II-era Junkers Ju 88 and North American B-25 Mitchell bombers had wingspans of 68 and 67 feet, respectively.

The German bombers had a respectable top speed of about 80 miles per hour, a ceiling of close to 17,000 feet, a bombload of 600 pounds, and a flying duration of almost five hours. Given that aviation had only just emerged from its infancy, these

Bombers Over England

In 1916, the German High Command was faced with an extraordinary dilemma. The weapon on which Germany had prided itself, the Zeppelin, had been introduced as a war-winning solution, one that perfectly expressed the triumph of Teutonic technology over Britain. Yet the Zeppelins were not obtaining results commensurate with the great cost of building and operating them, both of which consumed prohibitively vast amounts of money and manpower, as well as such precious materials as aluminum and rubber. Furthermore, British air defense systems were improving to the point that only raids under the most favorable conditions had a chance of success.

Yet German military chiefs could not bring themselves to simply abandon attacks on England. To do so would constitute an admission of failure, which the British would no doubt convert into a propaganda victory. This could not be endured. The Germans therefore turned to the new Gotha bomber aircraft, which, it was decided, would first supplement, and then perhaps replace, the Zeppelin.

In 1917 General Ernst von Hoeppner was given command of the newly established *Luftstreitkraft*—Combtant Air Forces. Hoeppner concluded that although Zeppelin raids on England were no longer productive, a new squadron equipped with 30 Gotha G IV bombers would yield results. In Hoeppner's view, a single Gotha carrying 600 pounds of bombs would be as effective as three Zeppelins. Hoeppner's plan was approved at the highest levels, and given the code name "Turkenkreuz" (Turk's Cross). In the midst of their bloody travail at Verdun, the Germans provided the wherewithal to create *Kampfgeschwader* (bomber squadron) 3, manned by the

German ground crew "bombs up" a Gotha.

elite of the Kaiser's bombing squadrons. Captain Ernst Brandenburg, a true soldier's soldier, was tabbed for command of the new squadron.

There was no ambiguity in Brandenburg's charter, even if the High Command overestimated the capability of bombing to bear on the outcome of the war. In essence, Brandenburg's Gothas were to "lay the basis for peace by intimidating the morale of the English people, and crushing their will to fight." He was, in addition, to disrupt the British war industry, disorganize communications, attack supply dumps, hinder transportation, attack shipping—the list went on. The General Staff officer who wrote the charter probably blotted it, sent it on, and then went out to have a glass of schnapps, certain that his efforts had all but won the war for Germany.

Brandenburg knew better. The Gothas were slow to arrive, and full of defects when they did. Brandenburg used the delay to modify the aircraft with an additional gravity fuel tank in the upper wing so that his aircraft could carry enough fuel to fly other than a direct route to England.

From May 25, 1917, to May 20, 1918, the Gothas made 297 sorties against targets in England; these missions were augmented by 28 sorties by the less famous, but even larger, R–planes. The German bomber force dropped almost 250,000 pounds of bombs, killed 835 British citizens, and injured another 1,972. Moreover, they caused an estimated $7.5 million of damage— paltry figures in comparison with the havoc wreaked by the large scale air raids of World War II, but of incalculable significance at the time.

Gothas were never employed in great numbers; the largest air raid involved a mere 28 aircraft. Nevertheless, the Gotha attacks had far-reaching consequences for Britain that extended to the end of the First World War and beyond. By 1918, the German bombers had drawn 11 RFC squadrons from the Western Front, caused the deployment of hundreds of antiaircraft guns and barrage balloons, and precipitated a political crisis in the British government, which in turn resulted almost directly in the creation of the Royal Air Force as an independent service arm. The Gothas had, moreover, forced into being a sophisticated air defense system that would, after undergoing two decades of evolution and improvements, defeat another German air offensive during the Battle of Britain in the summer and fall of 1940.

The psychological damage inflicted by the Gothas was slow to heal, and of lasting significance for the future of Germany. The British would not soon forget what the German bombers had done to their country; and they would exact a terrible vengeance for Gotha raids in the bombing offensive conducted by Air Marshall Sir Arthur Harris' Bomber Command in World War II. The seeds sewn by the Gotha's bombing reaped not a whirlwind but a firestorm for the Third Reich. (For a fascinating insight into Germany's First World War bombing operations, see *The Sky on Fire* by Raymond H. Fredette.)

are impressive figures. The G II even stacks up well against later aircraft like Britain's Keystone LB-5 bombers, which appeared some ten years later. The Keytone had a top speed of only 109 mph, a service ceiling of only 8,000 feet, and a range of 435 miles. Thus, aside from a bomb load capacity of 2,132 pounds, the Keystone was not markedly superior to the Gotha.

The Gotha was of conventional wood and fabric construction, with the fuselage being covered in plywood. For crews crossing the English Channel it was some comfort that the fuselage was waterproof and theoretically capable of remaining afloat for several hours. A ring mounting in the nose carried a Parabellum machine gun for the front gunner, while one or two more machine guns were provided for rear defense. One gun was installed in a ring mounting for attacks from the side and above, and could be depressed to fire through a plywood-sheathed tunnel in the bottom of the aircraft's fuselage. A number of Allied aircraft were lost to this "stinger" until its capability became well known. On rare occasions, a fourth crew member was carried to operate a gun placed in the bottom rear of the fuselage.

The Gotha was relatively well equipped, and used perhaps the best bombsight of the war, the Goerz, which had a three-foot long telescope as a part of its assembly. Two cylinders of compressed oxygen were carried, the crew members drawing on the oxygen directly from a pipe-stem fitting. Because the effects of altitude were not fully understood—and because the crews were all young men, full of beans—a flask of cognac was often used as a preferred substitute for pure oxygen, which parched the throat.

As large and as capable as they were, the Gothas, like the Zeppelins, had their share of negative features. They proved to be relatively frail aircraft, susceptible to damage if not landed on a prepared surface. Their Mercedes engines had many defects stemming from material shortages in Germany. And, as was the case with all other twin engine aircraft of the time, the Gotha could not fly on one engine. In the event of single engine failure, the aircraft's glide could be extended somewhat by applying full

Resembling a species of flying dinosaur, a Staaken R VI *Reisenflugzeug* ("giant plane") lumbers into the air. Less famous than the Gotha, the R VI was larger and carried a heavier bomb load.

power to the remaining good engine; nevertheless, when an engine quit over England, the crews usually suffered one of two fates, neither of them pleasant: capture or death, both of which could occur after a crash-landing, or a descent into the chilly waters of the English Channel or the North Sea.

Engine failure, inclement weather, and the sheer enormity of the task at hand resulted in a high accident rate. Only 24 Gothas were shot down while 36 were lost in non-combat mishaps.

Oddly enough, while the Gotha was relatively pleasant to fly when fully loaded, as the load decreased it became progressively unstable, and thus much more difficult to control. This often made the return from a mission as dicey as the mission itself. More than one Gotha was lost on the landing approach when the pilot, already exhausted by combat and a long round-trip flight over water and enemy territory, lacked the strength to manhandle his wayward aircraft onto the ground.

Part of the stability problem was due to contemporary construction techniques. It must be remembered that all aircraft of the period were kept in trim through a system of braces, turnbuckles, and wires that needed constant adjustment. A change in the weather, a rainstorm, or simple neglect could cause vast differences in its flying qualities as the wood and fabric surfaces twisted

out of shape. Proper maintenance was frequently lacking, since aircraft mechanics often received hurried, inadequate, training, and because the continual demand for infantry troops depleted the rear echelon units from which mechanics were drawn. A good mechanic became as highly prized as a good pilot.

The Gothas were joined in battle by the little known, but even more impressive R-planes, the *Riesenflugzeug* (giant aircraft). These aircraft were aptly named; one of them, the Staaken R VI, had four 260 horsepower Mercedes engines and a wingspan of just under 138 feet. (The Boeing B-29 Superfortress, the monster aircraft of World War II, only just exceeded this figure with a wingspan of 141 feet!). The R VI also had a loaded weight of 25,269 pounds, and could carry 2,400 pounds of bombs on missions lasting eight hours. Top speed was 80 miles per hour. Few R-planes were actually built, and only five of the Giants flew over England at one time. The damage they did was more psychological than actual. Yet such damage should not be discounted. To be sure, the casualties caused by the Gothas and Giants were trivial in number compared to the daily slaughter on the Western Front (see sidebar). But these losses came at home, in England, and were largely civilian. As a result, the German air raids had a truly profound impact on the collective psyche of the British populace.

M. Hagel

Fokker Eindecker

The first air superiority fighter was not so superior after all

In the seesaw struggle that characterized the war on, and above, the Western Front, 1915 stands out as killing time for German pilots, and a time of death for their Allied counterparts. During this period, numerous slow British and French observation planes became "Fokker fodder," helpless victims of a seemingly invincible little monoplane fighter that spat lead through its propeller arc.

But the Eindecker was something of a fraud. Just as the de Havilland DH-4 had an undeserved reputation for bursting into flames, so too was the Fokker Eindecker undeservedly regarded as the master fighter plane—faster, more maneuverable, and far more deadly than anything flown by the Allies. In fact, the DH-4 didn't burn any more often or readily than other contemporary observation planes; and the Eindecker was a terribly ordinary aircraft. But, for a brief

Main image, left: Like birds of prey closing in for the kill, a pair of Fokker Eindeckers swoop past a British Vickers F.B.5 "Gunbus" in a painting by Mike Hagel. The Eindecker made first use of a synchronized machine gun. *Above:* Anthony Fokker, creator of the Eindecker, is shown here with his M 18 Z biplane.

FOKKER EINDECKER

Above: The advent of improved Allied aircraft, designed specifically to counter the Fokker scourge, spurred the Germans to upgrade the single-gun armament of early Eindecker models. A special E IV (*above*) with a Le Rhone engine and three guns was prepared for Max Immelmann, who was to lose his life in the type. The Standard E IV (*right*) was armed with twin machine guns.

spell, it exceeded its limitations by virtue of a device that revolutionized aerial warfare: a machine gun synchronized to fire forward between the spinning blades of the propeller.

The Eindecker's creator, Anthony Fokker, was a great pilot, a fair designer, and a magnificent salesman. He was also a man who sometimes played fast and loose with the historical record, especially when discussing his own aircraft. In his autobiography, for instance, he conveys the impression that the design for the Eindecker sprang fully formed from his brain, and that his invention of the synchronized machine gun occurred within the space of 48 hours.

This is utter nonsense. Fokker's claims to the contrary, the Eindecker's creation was a complex process that owed much to luck, inspiration, and hard work. It also benefited from Fokker's policy of helping himself liberally to ideas that were not his own. In 1912, for instance, he was greatly influenced by the Morane-Saulnier monoplane, a copy of which he acquired and disassembled for study. His chief engineers, Martin Kruetzer and Rheinhold Platz, improved on the Morane-Saulnier to create the Fokker M.5, the direct ancestor of the Eindecker.

The Eindecker's synchronized machine gun also had a more complicated origin than Fokker cared to admit. In March 1915, a famous French pilot, Roland Garros, had equipped his Morane-Saulnier monoplane with a propeller protected by angled steel armor plates mounted on its base. Garros had placed an unsynchronized gun to fire through the propeller, bravely allowing those bullets that hit the prop to be deflected by the steel plates. In this manner Garros had racked up four victories when, on April 19, an ancient German reservist made the rifle shot of a lifetime, cutting the French pilot's fuel line and forcing him to land behind German lines, where his secret was discovered.

The Germans evaluated the deflector device, and demanded that Fokker install a similar one on the Eindecker. Fokker demurred. He preferred instead to concentrate his efforts on the development of a synchronization device, which would use an interrupter gear to fire the machine gun's bullets between the propeller blades. Although he later claimed to have invented the device himself, it was probably developed by his engineers from pre-existing patents (a similar device had been patented before the war by a German named Franz Schneider).

Trials of the device were so successful that an order was placed for 50 Fokker aircraft, each of them mounting a single synchronized machine gun. The most numerous version was the E III, a tiny plane weighing 1,232 pounds, with a wingspan of 31 feet, two-and-three-quarters inches, and a top speed of 88 miles per hour. Powered by a 100-horsepower Oberursel rotary engine, it used wing warping for lateral control, and was armed with one synchronized machine gun. (Later, some pilots mounted two and even three guns, an expedient that increased firepower but severely degraded aircraft performance.)

Employed singly along a wide expanse of front, the Eindeckers were an immediate success, especially in the hands of such superb pilots as lieutenants Max Immelmann and Oswald Boelcke. Both men were to become aces and be awarded the Pour le Mérite (popularly known as the Blue Max—the medal bestowed on Germany's bravest airmen); and both were to die in aviation accidents. But not before Eindecker pilots had inflicted the "Fokker scourge" on the Allies, scoring numerous victories and establishing air superiority over the Western Front.

The Eindecker's reign was short-lived, however. The Allies quickly responded with such planes as the Nieuport 11, which mounted a machine gun on the upper wing to fire over the propeller; and the de Havilland D.H.2, a pusher aircraft (with the propeller facing to the rear) that mounted a fixed, forward-firing machine gun in the nose. Both aircraft outclassed the Eindecker, enabling the Allies to temporarily regain air superiority in the first half of 1916. The Fokker scourge was over.

Lockheed Vega

In the 1920s and '30s, the Vega was the aircraft of choice—and accomplishment—for daring aviators.

Even among aircraft that are regarded as classics, the Lockheed Vega stands out as something special. The Vega had everything and did everything. Fast, with elegant lines enhanced by obvious strength, the Vega attracted many of the best pilots of the era—Wiley Post, Jimmie Mattern, Amelia Earhart, Roscoe Turner, and Sir Hubert Wilkins, to name but a few. Yet, so docile were its flying characteristics, lesser pilots also won fame in the Vega. Vegas flew the oceans, explored the Arctic and Antarctic, and circumnavigated the globe; they were the mainstay of airlines, ran bootleg whisky, flew movie stars to Reno, and were themselves featured in numerous motion pictures. Decades later a Vega would become a "stealth classic," recalled from retirement to serve as a radar test-bed because its wooden structure had such low radar reflectivity.

Curiously, the very advanced lines of the Vega belied the fact that its basic technology was of the World War I era. Designer Jack Northrop had adapted the methods he and the Loughead brothers had used in 1919 for the construction of their little S-1, a plywood monocoque fuselage formed under pressure in concrete molds. He added a wing very much like those used for years by Anthony Fokker, only enclosing the old wine of Fokker's construction techniques in the new bottle of a streamlined shape.

Equipped with the new Wright air-cooled, 220-horsepower engine, the first Vega was designed to carry five people at a top speed of 135 mph. But that was just for starters. The Vega matured over time, becoming ever faster and more capable, eventually serving as the basis for six other Lockheed aircraft—each one entitled to be considered a classic on its own.

In today's world of multi-billion dollar aircraft deals, automated factories, and thousand-person engineering teams, it is refreshing to note that the Lockheed Aircraft Corporation, which was formed in Nevada on December 17, 1926, got started with a paid-in capital of only $25,000. The company's first factory was a ramshackle plant in Hollywood, California, at the corner of Sycamore and Romaine streets—a bare bones building where clear-glass incandescent lights were strung between the rafters on long cords. The engineering staff was very small, yet extraordinarily capable, with Northrop, as Chief of Design, ably assisted by Gerry Vultee, soon to be a famous aircraft manufacturer in his own right.

Lockheed could not have come into being at a better time. On May 21, 1927, Charles Lindbergh landed in

Left, top: Blueprint in hand, Jack Northrop points out the features of the Vega to the Loughead brothers, Malcolm (*center*) and Allen. Behind them is a Vega under construction. *Left:* Captain George Wilkins (*left*) and Carl Ben Eielson with their Vega before embarking on the 1928 transpolar flight. *Above:* Frank Hawks and the Texaco Air Express, a parasol-wing Vega with the cockpit positioned aft of the passenger compartment.

Above: Amelia Earhart enhanced her reputation as America's "First Lady of the Air" in a Vega Model 5C. Here Earhart and Lockheed executives Allen Loughead, Carl Squier, and Lloyd Stearman stand in front of the aircraft she later flew to aviation renown. *Main image, right:* Cutaway painting by John Batchelor of the "Winnie Mae," perhaps the most famous Vega of them all. Owned by Texas oilman F.C. Hall, Winnie Mae is more commonly associated with pilot Wiley Post, who achieved several aviation firsts in the elegant plane.

Paris after completing his famous solo flight across the Atlantic, thereby sparking an explosively dynamic period in aviation. Less than two months later, on July 4, veteran test pilot Eddie Bellande made the first test flight in a Vega, taking off from a dusty field at what is now a corner of Los Angeles International Airport. The Vega, which had an open cockpit, exhibited classic performance characteristics from the start, amazing Bellande with its combination of speed and easy handling.

Even at that early stage in its development, the Vega had found a buyer—publisher George Hearst, Jr., who paid $12,000 for the plane. Hearst entered his Vega in what became known as the Dole Derby, a race from Oakland to Hawaii that was scheduled to begin on August

16, 1927. Named the "Golden Eagle," this first Vega was equipped with every known safety device—radios, earth inductor compass, floatation bags, life rafts, and signal flares. The open cockpit was faired-in with triplex glass, and the entire airplane was given a bright orange paint job. The odds-makers had reckoned it a shoo-in to win, but such was not to be the case. Somewhere between the California coast and its mid-Pacific destination the Golden Eagle vanished, never to be seen again.

Lockheed suffered no ill effects from the Golden Eagle's disappearance. On the contrary, the company was besieged by orders for the Vega. Lockheed completed two more models in 1927. In the meantime, Jack Northrop, anticipating continued business success, began designing the

Vega's low-wing and parasol-wing successors, and even had visions of a flying wing dancing in his richly creative mind.

Among the first besides Hearst to purchase a Vega was Captain George H. Wilkins (later Sir Hubert Wilkins), an Australian who wanted to use the plane to explore the Arctic. He and Carl Ben Eielson took off from Point Barrow on August 15, 1928, and flew across the roof of the world to Spitzbergen, Norway, in 20 hours. The following year, a team of flyers led by Wilkins took two Vegas to Antarctica, and there mapped 100,000 square miles of previously unexplored territory.

The Arctic and Antarctic flights demonstrated that the Vega's flying capabilities were as good as its looks. Lockheed's order book filled accord-

ingly, necessitating a move to a new location in Burbank, and an expansion to a 50-person work force. Even so, the Lockheed crew was hard-pressed to keep up with the demand for the Vega.

In an era of record-setting flights, the Vega became the aircraft of choice—and accomplishment—for daring aviators. Art Goebel (who had won the Dole Derby in a Travel Air monoplane) teamed with sportsman Harry Tucker for a nonstop flight across the United States in the "Yankee Doodle," a glistening white Vega decked out with red and blue speed-stripes, and powered by a 425-horsepower Pratt & Whitney Wasp engine. The Wasp doubled the power previously available to the Vega, enabling a top speed of 185 miles per hour, while showing to good effect

the strength and versatility of the Vega's structure. Goebel and Tucker flew from Los Angeles to Long Island in 18 hours, 58 minutes, a transcontinental speed record. The speedy Yankee Doodle was the first aircraft to make such a trip in less than 24 hours, and the first to fly nonstop from the west coast to the east.

Nowadays, air travel is such a commonplace occurrence that it is difficult to imagine the star-status accorded flyers like Goebel, as well as the intense competition among the pilots for records. This competition was abetted and intensified by exhaustive newspaper and newsreel coverage—all of which stimulated Vega sales.

Northrop and Lockheed were quite willing to satisfy the varying needs of their customers, even to the extent of

radically modifying the Vega. An example of this was the Air Express, built by Lockheed for the Texaco oil company. The Air Express had its wing mounted on struts, parasol fashion, and had the pilot's open cockpit positioned behind the passenger compartment. It was also fitted with the first of the new NACA (National Advisory Committee for Aeronautics) full-length engine cowlings, which smoothed the flow of air across the nose of the aircraft, while at the same improving engine cooling so the engine could be run safely at higher power settings. The NACA cowlings were a technological leap forward that was to have great impact not only on Vega performance, but on the performance of all military and commercial aircraft powered by radial engines.

Wiley Post: The Dashing Pilot in the White Vega

"It takes a Lockheed to beat a Lockheed."

In the early 1930s, that slogan pretty much summed up the state of aviation, and aircraft development, as it then existed. That Lockheed aircraft were seen to be so clearly superior to all but their own kind was due in large measure to Wiley Post. In the six years between his work as a production test pilot for Lockheed to his death in an aviation accident with humorist Will Rogers, Post blazed new aviation trails as a pilot—and, oddly enough, as a scientist.

Post was an certainly an unlikely candidate for scientific achievement. A former Oklahoma oil field roustabout, he had taken up flying after losing an eye in a job-related accident, using insurance money to pay for lessons. Despite the limitations it imposed on his vision, Post's injury did nothing to inhibit his considerable flying skills. Employed as the personal pilot for F. C. Hall, a wheeler-dealer in oil leases, he put these skills to good use at the controls of the "Winnie Mae," an all-white Vega named after Hall's daughter. In 1930, Hall sponsored Post and the Winnie Mae in the National Air Races, a nonstop event that went from Burbank to Chicago. Post was a dark horse in a field of stellar contenders like Roscoe Turner, Art Goebel, Billy Brock, and Lee Schoenhair—all flying Lockheeds, incidentally—but he won the race anyway, completing the course in nine hours, nine minutes.

Shortly thereafter, Post decided to have a go at the round-the-world travel record previously set by the German dirigible *Graf Zeppelin*. Six months of careful preparation ensued. Then, on June 23, 1931, Post and his navigator, Harold Gatty, took off in the Winnie Mae from Roosevelt Field, Long Island—the traditional starting place for so many aviation exploits prior to this one. The *Graf Zeppelin* had circumnavigated the globe in 21 days, seven hours, and 31 minutes; Post and Gatty completed the circuit (with 14 stops in between) in eight days, 15 hours, and 51 minutes!

Sporting a buccaneer's eye patch, Post cut quite the dashing figure as an aviator. Not surprisingly, the public adored him; he was the very image of a flying hero, a man who personified in look and deed all the romance and adventure of aviation. Post proved worthy of their adulation; he was not a pilot content to rest on his laurels.

Starting on July 15, 1933, he used an autopilot to help him circumnavigate the globe *solo* (again in the Winnie Mae), in just seven days, 18 hours, and 49 minutes.

Post next became preoccupied with high altitude work, during which he developed a pressure suit that was the progenitor of those used today by military pilots and astronauts. Flying at high altitudes, he was among the first humans to encounter the jet stream; and, in 1935, he attained a speed of 340 miles per hour during a transcontinental attempt. Unfortunately, that same flight ended in a crash landing that damaged the faithful Winnie Mae beyond repair.

Discouraged, Post and his friend Will Rogers embarked upon a flying holiday in a dangerously nose-heavy Lockheed floatplane. Lockheed engineers had warned Post about his hybrid lash-up of Orion, Sirius, and Explorer parts, but he didn't heed them. On August 15, 1935, Post's engine quit just after take-off from Point Barrow, Alaska, crashing on its back and killing both men instantly. The dashing pilot with the eye patch was dead; but his name, and the name of the Winnie Mae, had earned a permanent and honored place in aviation history.

Wiley Post and the Winnie Mae. Note the distance records listed on the fuselage. Following his around-the-world flight in 1933, Post used Winnie Mae to conduct high altitude research. Wearing a specially fabricated pressurized suit, he ascended to an unofficial altitude record of over 50,000 feet in December 1934.

Air-racer Roscoe Turner with his parasol-wing Vega, called "Gilmore" after his oil company sponsor. (Turner's pet lion, also named Gilmore, inspired the fuselage art.)

The Air Express was a marketing tool, used by Texaco to garner publicity for its products. The company's paid pilot-in-residence was the aptly named Frank Hawks. On February 4, 1929, Hawks teamed with Oscar Grubb in an attempt to set a new west-to-east transcontinental speed record. Grubb was more than a passenger—he was also the manual labor component, working in a fume-laden environment to pump gasoline from tins located in the cabin into the aircraft's fuel tanks. It was a harrowing flight during which Grubb was nearly overcome by fumes and Hawks several times lost his way. Nevertheless, when they landed the Air Express in New York, they had somehow managed to shave 30 minutes from the record set by Goebel and Tucker.

Lockheed built a total of 130 Vegas, as well as 68 variants (such as the Air Express) closely derived from the

Charles Lindbergh's Sirius was a derivative of the Vega design, and equipped with floats. In 1931 Lindbergh and his wife, Anne, used the Sirius to survey a prospective air route across the Pacific for Pan Am.

Vega design. Many of the greatest names in aviation came to be associated with the Lockheed aircraft. Charles Lindbergh and his wife Anne flew one of the variants, the low-wing Sirius, on route exploration trips for Pan American; Wiley Post (see sidebar) piloted a Vega called the "Winnie Mae;" and Amelia Earhart owned and operated a gorgeous Vega Model 5.

Earhart had taken possession of her red and gold Lockheed in 1930. On May 20, 1932, she piloted the air-craft from Newfoundland to Northern Ireland in 15 hours, 18 minutes, becoming the first woman to fly solo across the Atlantic. Three months later, in the same airplane, she flew from New York to Los Angeles, becoming the first woman to make a solo nonstop transcontinental flight, and setting a speed record of 19 hours, five minutes in the process.

After that feat Amelia Earhart was proclaimed "America's First Lady of the Air" and her red and gold Vega was enshrined in the Franklin Institute in Philadelphia. (It is now on exhibit in the National Air and Space Museum.) She acquired another Vega, also painted it red and gold, and proceeded with her assault on the record books. On January 11, 1935, she flew from Hawaii to California in 18 hours, 16 minutes. She thus became the first woman to fly nonstop across both the Atlantic and the Pacific—and she had made both flights in Lockheed Vegas.

Amelia Earhart went on to set many records in her Vega. Her most ambitious undertaking unfortunately proved to be her last. It was not to be made in a Vega, however. In 1937 Earhart and copilot Fred Noonan were lost in the Pacific after completing two-thirds of a round-the-world flight in a Lockheed L-10 Electra, a twin-engine successor to the Vega.

Jimmie Mattern's Vega 5C sported a gaudy, bird-of-prey paint scheme. Mattern made many famous long-distance flights, then went on to become a top pilot with Lockheed.

Curtiss Racers

When the '20s were roaring, they roared to victory

Among the more glorious aircraft of the 1920s were the racers developed between 1921 and 1925 by the Curtiss Aeroplane and Engine Company of Long Island. The sleek biplanes in this series were used by both the Navy and the Army, and provided the foundation for a complete line of fighters and engines that culminated in the beautiful Curtiss P-6E.

The competitions in which they participated, and excelled, were more than mere trials of speed; they were also the laboratories and proving grounds for many key advances in aircraft development. As such, they became headline-grabbing events where beautifully built planes from Britain, France, Italy, and the United States became the instruments by which international aviation prestige was acquired or lost, as the case may be. Naturally, the races were watched closely by the governments of the aforementioned countries, for the prestige that came with winning could translate into tremendous financial gain in the aircraft sales market.

The United States upset the international applecart with its fleet of Curtiss racers, which dominated the competition for five years running. Although improved and modified every year, particularly through the installation of more powerful engines, the basic formula for the Curtiss racers remained the same: single seat, open cockpit biplanes with frames as streamlined as contemporary aviation technology would allow.

The first two planes of the series were retroactively designated CR-1 and CR-2. Flying a CR-2, a Navy pilot named Bert Acosta won the 1921 Pulitzer Trophy race (sponsored by the Pulitzer brothers of publishing fame) with an average speed of 176.7 miles per hour. An Army variant, designated R-6, had an uprated engine and the sensational new Curtiss wing-surface radiators, which greatly

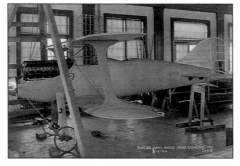

The R-6 under construction in the Curtiss factory. The sleek biplane was powered by the revolutionary new Curtiss D-12 engine.

reduced drag; thus modified, and with Lieutenant Russell Maughan at the controls, the aircraft claimed the 1922 Pulitzer at a sizzling 205.8 miles per hour. Four days later Brigadier General Billy Mitchell used the same plane to set a world's speed record of 224.28 miles per hour.

The CR-1s and CR-2s were subsequently modified and given a new designation, CR-3. Equipped with floats and a 475-horsepower engine, a Navy CR-3 flown by Lieutenant David Rittenhouse won the prestigious Schneider Trophy race (sponsored by Frenchman Jacque Schneider) in 1923 at 177.4 miles per hour. It was America's first Schneider race victory. Also in 1923, another Navy pilot, Lieutenant Al Williams, won the Pulitzer race at 243.68 miles per hour in an R2C-1, a much improved version of the R-6.

The United States could have won permanent possession of the Schneider Trophy in 1924, when it was the only nation able to field a racing team in the competition; instead, however, it gallantly agreed to postpone the race until the following year. It is interesting to note that Britain, when faced with the same opportunity in 1931, elected to fly their Supermarine racers around the course to an uncontested victory. The British thus laid permanent claim to the trophy, but in so doing tarnished their reputation for sportsmanlike conduct.

Bert Acosta leans against his Curtiss R-1 after winning the 1921 Schneider race. Standing on the ground in front of him is the Schneider cup.

Above: Lt. Jimmy Doolittle stands on the float of an Army R3C-2 at Baltimore. Doolittle won the 1925 Schneider race in a sistership of this plane. *Right*: Cyrus Bettis poses with his R3C-1, in which he won the 1925 Pulitzer race.

In 1925 the Army and Navy jointly purchased three racers, the R3C series. Lieutenant Cyrus Bettis, an Army pilot, won the Pulitzer race, coaxing 248.9 miles per hour out of his plane. Another Army pilot, the incomparable Jimmy Doolittle, then enjoyed upstaging a Navy entrant in the Schneider Trophy race, flying a float-equipped R3C-2 to win at 245.7 miles per hour. The R3C-2 may still be seen today, in the National Air and Space Museum, a glistening gold-and black tribute to one of the greatest line of racers in history.

Douglas DC-3

A true aircraft immortal,
the DC-3 just keeps on flying

The Douglas DC-3 is an aircraft capable of inspiring an affection bordering on the mystical among aviation enthusiasts. Loved by its pilots, its passengers, its mechanics, and even by the enemies of the nation that produced it, the DC-3 began life as the most advanced transport in history, and continues to be used today for tasks that other, more modern, aircraft cannot perform. Today, DC-3s are not only in productive service, they are in experimental programs designed to further their use and lengthen their life span. In every respect, the DC-3 is *the* classic among classics.

The most successful piston engine transport plane of all time traces its origins to an intense competition between United Airlines and TWA (which was then called Transcontinental and Western Airlines). United—then part of an enormous holding company that included Boeing, Pratt & Whitney, Hamilton Standard, and other aviation powerhouses—had garnered sole production of Boeing's sensational new Model 247 transports, which entered service in 1933. The Model 247 had revolutionized air

transportation with its all-metal low-wing monoplane construction and retractable landing gear; in the process, it had also rendered obsolete every other airliner then flying, including the venerable Ford and Fokker trimotors.

United Airlines thus had the wherewithal to seize commericial air supremacy from its competitors. In response to this threat, Jack Frye, TWA Vice President in Charge of Operations (and a famous flyer in his own right), urgently contacted five aircraft manufacturers: Curtiss, Consolidated, General Aviation, Martin, and Douglas. Frye asked each manufacturer to submit a proposal for a 12-passenger, all metal, trimotor airliner with a cruising speed of 146 miles per hour—a formidable specification.

Due to a number of recent engineering developments, including the NACA cowling pioneered on the Vega, Douglas was confident that it could exceed all of TWA's requirements with a twin engine design. Douglas persuaded TWA likewise, but only after a series of forceful discussions, and only after the aircraft

manufacturer agreed to a bombshell of a stipulation; namely, that the new airliner had to be able to take off fully loaded on one engine from any airport in TWA's network.

This was indeed a challenge, for no twin engine aircraft yet built had such a capability. Legend has it that the brilliant Douglas design team (led by Donald Douglas himself, and including such magnificent engineers as James H. "Dutch" Kindleberger and Arthur E. Raymond), placed a drawing of the Boeing Model 247 over its engineering tables inscribed with the motto "Like This, Only Better." Less than ten months after the contract was signed, on July 1, 1933, the Douglas Commercial Number One, or DC-1, took to the air. On September 4, the DC-1 took off from Winslow, Arizona, and flew to Albuquerque, New Mexico, with one engine shut down from take-off to landing—thus satisfying the TWA requirement.

The DC-1 was, in truth, "like" the Boeing 247—both were all-metal, low-wing monoplanes with retractable landing gears—but it was in almost every way better. The Douglas aircraft was faster, carried more passengers, and, more importantly, offered the opportunity for growth.

And grow it did, almost immediately. The DC-1 met all contractual requirements and more, but the Douglas design team, its confidence bolstered by results, redesigned the production aircraft into the 14-passenger DC-2, which was capable of an unheard-of 18-hour transcontinental service. Airlines all over the world, including United, began to order the silver beauty from Santa Monica.

If the series had ended with the DC-2 it would still have been an unqualified success, for 193 of the type (including military versions) were built, and served with distinction all over the world. (One has to

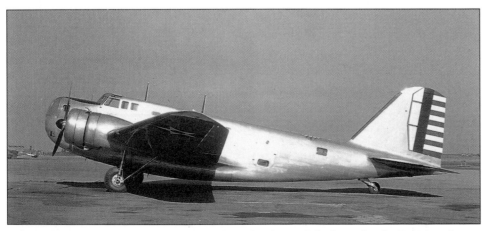

Above: The DC-2, a predecessor of the DC-3, also formed the basis for the B-18 bomber (nicknamed "Bolo"), one of which is shown here in 1937. *Opposite page:* The *Elkins*, flagship DC-3 of American Airlines, is parked next to another classic, a 1941 Ford Club Coupe. By the early 1940s, DC-3s comprised 80 percent of the passenger planes then in service with American carriers.

Above: The one and only DC-1, shown here in TWA markings, had several owners before going to Republican Spain in 1938 during the Spanish Civil War. In December 1940 it was written off after a crash landing in Malaga.

Right: Although overshadowed by the later DC-3, the DC-2 (shown here) was an extraordinary aircraft in its own right, revolutionizing air transport design throughout the world. Able to carry 14 passengers across the continental United States in a mere 18 hours, the DC-2 quickly became a much sought-after item by foreign as well as domestic airlines.

Above: This 1940s-vintage postcard depicts a DC-2 belonging to Eastern Airlines' "Great Silver Fleet" flying low over the tall buildings of downtown Houston, Texas.

remember that 193 transport aircraft represented, for its era, a high production volume—so high that Douglas felt compelled to recruit workers from the Boeing plant in Seattle. Many of the ex-Boeing employees were snuff-taking Swedish immigrants, who allowed themselves to be lured away to the Douglas plant on condition that spittoons be placed on the production line floor.) The DC-2 also formed the basis for the Douglas B-18 "Bolo" bomber, which was itself not a great advance as a combat machine, but which served with distinction in Alaska, and as an antisubmarine patrol aircraft.

Since an 18-hour transcontinental flight could be wearing to travelers accustomed to the relative luxury of a Pullman sleeper, the newly formed American Airlines (formerly American Airways) asked Douglas to develop a sleeper transport. Douglas was initially reluctant to comply with this request, as it was having difficulty enough fulfilling DC-2 orders. But a Douglas design team led by Raymond, and including Ed Burton, Lee Atwood, and Bailey Oswald, quickly converted the basic DC-2 design to a "wide body" configuration by making the fuselage 26 inches wider. The DST, as this variant was designated, could thus accommodate a double berth on either side of the aisle. Lengthening the fuselage by two feet, six and 1/4 inches permitted the addition of a row of seats, and the fuselage contours were made more rounded and streamlined. To counter the resultant increase in gross weight, the DST's wings were strengthened and stretched to a 95-foot span, and the empennage (tail assembly) was also enlarged.

Compared to other passenger aircraft, the DST was incredibly sophisticated, boasting de-icers for propellers and wings, autopilots, cabin sound proofing, automatic fire extinguishers, duplicate controls for the copilot, and controllable pitch propellers. However, since Douglas was a conservative firm, the DC-3, like its predecessors, would retain a gear retraction system that left part of the wheel exposed to facilitate a belly landing in case the pilot forgot to extend the landing gear.

The first DST flew on December 17, 1935. American Airlines had purchased ten DST's for $79,500 each—a considerable sum in the mid-1930s. The planes could carry 14 passengers at night in sleeping berths, or 28 passengers by day in somewhat cramped seating.

It was evident from the start to Douglas engineers that an alternative version of the DST, not equipped with berths, would be an even more attractive airplane than the DC-2. Thus the DC-3 was born. This plane was capable of carrying 21 passengers, a 50 percent payload increase over the DC-2. The additional payload capacity, when factored in with a 170-mile per hour cruising speed, made the DC-3 the first passenger airliner able to operate profitably on its passenger traffic alone, without government subsidy.

The DST flies over Central Park in New York in April 1939. The right propeller is feathered (i.e., engine shut down with propeller blade perpendicular to line of flight) to demonstrate the plane's ability to fly on one engine.

A Japanese Tabby, photographed by the gun-camera of a low-flying American plane in July 1944. Essentially a DC-3, the Tabby was built in Japan by Nakajima and Showa for use by the Japanese navy.

The DC-3 in Foreign Service

It was inevitable that an airplane as advanced as the Douglas series of transports would be sought out by foreign users. Most acquired the DC-3 through normal (which is to say, legal) channels, by purchasing the aircraft outright or, in the case of the Soviet Union and Japan, by building the aircraft under license from Douglas. Some foreign users, however, got ownership of their DC-3s by unscrupulous means. Some manufacturers attempted to copy the design, building *faux* DC-3s that were decidedly inferior to the real thing. Other users, usually those hostile to the United States, acquired their DC-3s through capture, confiscation, impressment, or simple piracy.

A life in foreign lands was the destiny for even the first of the series, the solitary Douglas DC-1. After breaking the transcontinental speed record in 1935, the DC-1 was acquired for use by Howard Hughes on his round-the-world flight. But Hughes never used it, electing instead to buy the faster Lockheed Model 14. The DC-1 was sold to an exporting company and eventually reached Spain during the Spanish Civil War (1936-1939). Operated as a civil transport, it crash-landed at Malaga, there to end its days as a pile of wreckage on the airfield—an ignoble end to a significant aircraft.

The DC-2 model was eagerly sought by foreign airlines, including those of the Netherlands, Switzerland, Spain, Poland, Rumania, France, the Soviet Union, and Japan. Fokker built the DC-2 under license, and Lufthansa used ten captured aircraft in regular service. The Fins fitted a DC-2 with guns and bomb racks and used it successfully against the Soviets in the Winter War (1939-1940). Military versions of the DC-2 (the C-33, C-38, C-39, C-41, and C-42) were used extensively worldwide.

Of course, the DC-3/C-47 saw even wider service. The Soviets had obtained 22 DC-3s, two of which were to serve as production guides while a Soviet design team spent two years in the Douglas plant learning how to build the aircraft. The leader of the Soviet team was Boris Lisunov, who studied not only the aircraft itself, but its tooling and support equipment as well. Lisunov was ably assisted by Mikhail Guryevich—who later teamed with Artyem Mikoyan to become the "G" in MiG. The Soviet DC-3 variant was originally known as the PS-84 and, later, as the Lisunov Li-2. The Soviets built 2,930 DC-3s, using them for military purposes and as a civilian carrier for Aeroflot, the state-run airline.

In 1937, Japan purchased 20 U.S. DC-3s; these aircraft served Greater Japan Air Lines throughout World War II. In 1938, Mitsui and Company paid $90,000 for the rights to build and sell the DC-3. Mitsui was acting as a front, however; the real purchaser was the Japanese Navy. Ultimately, the Nakajima and Showa companies built 485 DC-3s, which were modified to accept Japanese engines and to compliment Japanese production techniques. Built in seven different versions, the airplane had the basic Japanese designation of L2D; the Allied code name for the aircraft was Tabby—a not unreasonable choice for a true pussycat of an airplane.

Silver Wings, Douglas C-47 - Over the Hump, by R.G. Smith: The military version of the DC-3, known officially as the Skytrain in U.S. service and the Dakota in British service, was almost always called the Gooney Bird. It is here depicted in an overflight of the Himalayan range during World War II. The C-47 was of inestimable value to the Allied cause, serving on literally every battlefront of the war. General Eisenhower, overall commander of Allied forces in Western Europe, declared that the C-47 was one of the five most important weapons of the war.

By 1941, over 80 percent of all American airliners were DC-3s. Moreover, DC-3s were so productive in passenger miles that they were carrying more than 90 percent of the world's airline traffic! Never before, and never since, has a single aircraft design cornered so much of the commercial aviation market.

World War II provided an added boost to the DC-3's career. In September 1940 the U.S. Army Air Corps ordered 146 C-47s, the military version of the DC-3. Within months additional orders poured in, and an unheard of quantity of planes—1,900—were ordered from a new facility being built in Oklahoma City.

The Army Air Corps became the United States Army Air Force in 1941, and the C-47 was designated "Skytrain"—one of those great-sounding names used only in advertisements. (The British called it the "Dakota," but the most appropriate and oft-used name was "Gooney Bird.") Ultimately more than 10,000 military versions of the C-47 (including the Navy R4-D) were built in the United States, a figure that indicates how important it was to the Allied cause, as well as the reason why it was cited by General Eisenhower as one of the five most important weapons of the war. Versions of the DC-3 were also built by the Soviet Union and even Japan (see sidebar).

The war showcased the incredible versatility of the basic DC-3 design. The airplane was used to carry paratroops, tow gliders, drop supplies, and ferry brass. It was fitted with huge EDO floats for water landings (and at this moment, a C-47 is being reequipped with the floats by restorers), and it had its engines removed to be tested as a glider. Designated XCG-17, the latter variant not surprisingly proved a better glider than any purpose-built aircraft of this type, and only the changing needs of the war kept it out of production.

As successful as the C-47 had been in World War II, few of its most ardent proponents could have predicted that it would emerge as an important aircraft five years later in the Korean War, and 19 years later in the Vietnam War. Yet it soldiered on with distinction in those conflicts. During the Vietnam War in particular, the C-47 became an important combat aircraft, serving as a gunship mounting fearsome multi-barrel Gatling guns. (The awesome destructive power of these guns, best seen at night when their tracer rounds poured down an unbroken stream of fire on enemy positions below, earned this C-47 variant the nicknames "Spooky" and "Puff the Magic Dragon.") In Vietnam the C-47 also served as a flare dropper, and as a psychological warfare airplane, the latter being equipped with loudspeakers to broadcast various messages and propaganda to any enemy soldiers that might be lurking in the area.

After World War II, thousands of C-47s became available as war surplus. They were promptly absorbed by the commericial aviation industry. Many small feeder airlines were started up with C-47s, which were relatively inexpensive compared to the cost of newer aircraft.

But aircraft manufacturers, Douglas included, believed that a replacement aircraft for the DC-3 was in order. There began an almost endless series

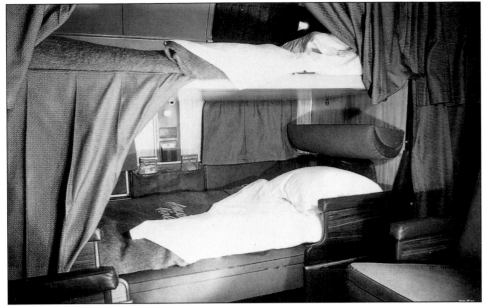

Above: Internal configurations of the DC-3 were myriad, and built according to public demand. This version featured sleeping berths on one side of the aisle, and conventional seating on the other.

Right: The blue-bordered national marking on the wing indicates that this photo of a C-47 loading cargo was taken after September 1943. The plane on the opposite side of the runway is a Boeing B-17G Flying Fortress.

Something of the strength and versatility of the DC-3's airframe is conveyed in this portrait of a DC-3 landing on an unimproved airstrip in America's desert Southwest. By contrast, modern jet airliners cannot land safely on unpaved runways.

Above: A C-47 zooms over coolies repairing an airstrip in China. Flying from India across the Himalayas, supply-laden C-47s helped to keep China in the war, and thus tie down over one million Japanese troops. *Below:* The Douglas Super DC-3 had better performance than the DC-3, which it was intended to replace. But the relatively high cost of the plane prevented it from gaining a foothold in the commercial marketplace.

of design studies for the "plane to replace the DC-3." Some of the aircraft produced by these efforts—such as the pressurized Convair 240 and Martin 404 series—enjoyed a modicum of success. Most, however, simply died on the drawing board. The fact was, on short hauls no airplane could do the job as well, or as economically as the DC-3. Even Douglas'

own DC-3 replacement, the Super DC-3, first flown in 1949, was unable to displace its predecessor. The Super DC-3 (also known as the R4-D8) was a cleaned up, more powerful version with markedly improved performance. But for commercial users the gains in performance were simply not worth the increase in cost.

The DC-3 was and remains a delightful aircraft to fly, forgiving, able to penetrate the worst weather and survive, and capable of carrying far greater loads than the designers had envisioned. Paradoxically, the DC-3's load-bearing capability and longevity is due in large measure to a *lack* of technology. The design team did not have access to computers; thus, when designing a part, Donald Douglas and his associates could not perfectly tailor its strength to an expected lifetime, or to an expected number of cycles. Instead, they designed the part to be strong enough to take care of any unforseen problems—and then beefed it up a little just for safety's sake. The result was an airplane with incredible longevity, and the related capability of endless modification.

Over the years, a number of attempts were made to adapt the basic DC-3 airframe to turbine power which would significantly boost the plane's performance. Most met with failure. It was found that the airframe could accept the strain imposed by turboprop engines, but being unpressurized, it could not carry passengers or live cargo at the altitudes where turboprops were most efficient. Basler Turbo Conversions Inc., an aircraft manufacturer located in Oshkosh, Wisconsin, has solved these problems by making extensive modifications to the fuselage and wings. The result of these efforts, dubbed BT-67 by Basler, is currently selling well in the world aviation market.

As evidenced by the BT-67 and numerous other variants, the DC-3 simply refuses to retire from the list of active aircraft. Indeed, more than five decades after the first DC-3s appeared, many standard versions of the aircraft are still in daily service, and several have been refurbished to provide nostalgic rides to passengers who recall the golden age when the DC-3 was king.

Main image, top: In *AC-47 Spooky Mission Near Saigon,* artist George Akimoto depicts the legendary Gatling gun-armed version of the C-47 pouring fire down on enemy positions during the Vietnam War. *Above, left:* Side view of the three multibarrel 7.62mm Gatling guns in the AC-47 gunship, also known as "Spooky" and "Puff the Magic Dragon." Each gun in the AC-47 was capable of firing *6,000* rounds per minute. *Above, right:* A Spooky on a mission over South Vietnam in October 1967.

Polikarpov I-16

The "Little Donkey" kicked more than a few enemy aircraft out of the sky

The Polikarpov I-16 achieved classic status at a time when the Soviet Union seemed, to many, to be incapable of producing anything worthwhile. In the years just preceding World War II, when the I-16 debuted, the Soviet Union was disparaged in the West as a technologically backward nation. It was believed that whatever advanced technology the Soviets possessed had been copied from Western sources rather than indigenously produced; and that these copies were themselves of inferior quality.

There was considerable truth to this view. But not when it was applied to the sphere of weaponry and weapons systems. For example, in the 1930s (and indeed, for many years thereafter) Soviet artillery, tanks, and aircraft were often equal, and in many instances superior to the same items produced in Europe and the United States.

Prior to the outbreak of World War II in 1939, the high quality of Soviet arms was already well known by the Soviet Union's adversaries: namely, Germany, Italy, and Japan. The armed forces of these three nations had fought against Soviet tanks and aircraft in conflicts ranging from Spain to Mongolia. To say the least, it had not been a pleasant experience: in the Spanish Civil War (1936-39), German and Italian expeditionary forces, sent to assist the Nationalist rebellion led by General Francisco Franco, were hard-pressed to overcome the Soviet-supplied Loyalist armies; and in the undeclared war that pitted Japan against the Soviet Union in the summer of 1939, Japan's vaunted Kwantung Army was severely trounced by Soviet forces in the Nomenhan region of Outer Mongolia.

Soviet aircraft had played an important role in both conflicts. They had proved their worth to their enemies; but not to the West. In the United States, the very aircraft the Japanese, Germans, and Italians had come to hold in high regard—the Polikarpov I-15 and I-16, and the Tupelov SB-2—were dismissed as poor imitations of, respectively, the Curtiss Hawk, the Boeing P-26, and the Martin B-10.

The facts were quite different. The I-15, although fully equivalent to the Hawk (and to the Gloster Gauntlet, Hawker Fury, Avia 534, to name but a few) resembled the American plane only superficially; like the Hawk, it was a biplane with a fixed landing gear and a radial engine. The SB-2's performance exceeded that of the

I-16s on a dirt airstrip in the Soviet Union. After proving themselves in combat in Spain and Mongolia, I-16s were called upon to defend Russia from invading Axis armies in the summer of 1941.

Top: A Po-2 converted for use as an airborne ambulance; note the wounded soldier on the stretcher. *Middle*: Predecessor to the I-16, the nimble I-15 entered service in 1934, and was used extensively by Republican forces in the Spanish Civil War. *Above*: The Boeing P-26 "Peashooter" bore a superficial resemblance to the I-16. In actuality, the I-16 was the superior airplane.

Martin B-10 by a considerable margin and it was built in far greater numbers; some 6,656 had been completed by 1941, whereas production of the Martin bombers did not exceed 336 units. And the I-16, far from being a copy of the P-26, was instead the vanguard of an aviation revolution.

That said, it should be noted that there was some basis for the belief that early Russian aircraft designs were copies. After the Bolshevik Revolution (1917), and the civil war that followed, the Soviet Union had been in a rush to create an industrialized socialist state. To speed the process, the Soviets quite logically chose to adapt the most suitable Western

designs to their own needs. N.N. Polikarpov, who would lead the I-16 design team, had cut his teeth on foreign aircraft, working during the upheaval of the civil war to build Soviet versions of the Spad S.VII and the de Havilland D.H.9A.

But Polikarpov and his fellow designers were not bound by this imitative approach. In an unfree society, they were free to experiment. And experiment they most certainly did. The very newness of the Soviet engineering culture—and the fact that state sponsorship eliminated concerns about competition—permitted departures in design that wouldn't occur elsewhere until a much later date. These departures resulted in the "gigantism" of some Soviet aircraft (such as designer Andrei Tupelov's enormous ANT 20 series), as well as a radical oddity like the Cheyeranovski Parabolic Wing. They were also responsible for the I-16.

In 1928 Polikarpov had scored his first major success with the design of the U-2 (subsequently designated Po-2 in his honor.) The U-2 was quite unlike the later Lockheed aircraft of the same designation, being a simple biplane trainer of about the same size, appearance, and complexity of a Consolidated PT-3. The U-2 was built in greater numbers than any other aircraft before *or* since; those numbers, however, vary considerably, ranging anywhere from 29,000 to 41,000 units produced.

Design work on the I-16 began during the summer of 1932 at the Central Aero and Hydrodynamic Institute. At this juncture Polikarpov was in the kind of straits that could only happen in the Soviet Union. His theretofore meteoric career, which had entailed a swift ascent to the top post of the OSS (the department for experimental land plane construction), had taken a sudden downward plunge upon the occasion of his arrest during the 1929 purge. Instead of a firing squad or a gulag, however, Polikarpov and his design team were sentenced to an "internal prison," there to continue their work under the close supervision and scrutiny of the state. Evidently, his prosecutors judged him too vital to the future of Soviet military prowess to inflict the usual penalties of summary execution or slow death in a labor camp.

An I-16 in flight, somewhere over the Eastern Front in World War II.

His was not a unique punishment; many other great Soviet designers received the same treatment, including Andrei Tupelov and Dimitrii Grigorovich.

(The success of the I-16 would later earn for Polikarpov a stay of sentence and repatriation into the comparative freedom of Soviet society. Polikarpov's subsequent designs were plagued with crashes, but having been blessed with Stalin's favor, he was immune to state retribution, which was directed instead at his colleagues. Polikarpov kept up his design work until 1944, when he collapsed and died of natural causes.)

In the event, the I-16 was developed in what most civilized societies would deem peculiar, if not abhorrent, circumstances. From the outset the idea was to create a low-wing monoplane fighter, a rather daring concept at a time when designers in more "advanced" nations were still attempting to refine the World War I formula of a two-gun, open cockpit, biplane fighter. The prototype (and all versions thereafter) was of mixed construction: the wing (which had a span of 29 feet, one and ⅔ inches) featured steel-tube spars and aluminum ribs, covered by flush riveted aluminum skin; while the fuselage was covered with plywood. Fitted with a 400-horsepower engine, the prototype first flew on December 31, 1933. It was immediately recognized to be of great promise, even though underpowered. A second prototype was flown on February 18, 1934, whereupon the aircraft was ordered into mass production.

The decision to build was made somewhat hastily, for both prototypes had exhibited many flaws. Some of these flaws would never be eliminated. Throughout its career, the I-16 was only marginally stable, and had a tendency to stall under even moderate G-loadings. And upon take-off, the pilot retracted the gear manually, which was accomplished through 44 turns of a small wheel. Each successive turn was more difficult to complete than the one before it, and as the pilot labored ever harder at his task, the cranking motion, transmitted through his body to the hand that held the control column, produced a corresponding wavy, or undulating, motion in the flight pattern of the ascending plane. When landing, the pilot had to maintain a relatively high power setting on the engine right up to the moment of touchdown; then, confronted by a possible loss of control, he had to perform a dance routine on the rudder pedals that would have been the envy of Fred Astaire.

But with all these shortcomings, the I-16 was *fast*. Early versions equipped with a 700-horsepower M-25 engine were capable of 280 miles per hour in *1934*. Later versions, powered by a 1,000-horsepower Shvetsove M-62 engine, gave it a maximum speed of 326 miles per hour at sea level. Moreover, in the hands of a good pilot the I-16 could be an exceptionally maneuverable aircraft. This combination of speed and maneuverability, combined with a heavy armament for the time (two 20 millimeter cannons and two 7.62 caliber machine guns), enabled the I-16 to perform with sufficient effec-

The stubby I-16 was originally designed as an air superiority fighter. Later in its career, it played an invaluable role as a bomber interceptor and ground attack plane.

tiveness to remain in front line service until the final months of 1942.

Some 20,000 I-16s were eventually built, and its widespread use on several of the world's major battlefronts earned it a variety of nicknames. The Spanish Nationalists called it *Mosca* (fly), while the Loyalists dubbed it *Rata* (rat); the Japanese termed it *Abu* (gadfly), while the Germans called it *Dienstjaeger* (duty fighter). To the Soviets, however, it became known as *Ishak*—"Little Donkey."

The Soviet name fit best. Like the donkey, the I-16 was both temperamental and hard-working; and, like the donkey, it was not much to look at. But then good looks, in and of themselves, don't count for much in combat. And the I-16 was no stranger to combat. It first saw action in the Spanish Civil War. Over 500 I-16s were sent to Spain, where the Soviet pilots that flew them used zoom and dive techniques to establish dominance over the German Heinkel He 51s and the Italian Fiat CR-32s.

In China and Mongolia the Ishaks also competed well with the Mitsubishi A5M "Claude" and Nakajima Type 97 "Nate" fighters flown by the Japanese; but in the Winter War of 1939-40, it enjoyed less success against Finland's Fokker D.XXIs and Brewster Buffalos. In the early stages of the war with Germany (which began, for the Soviets, in June 1941), the I-16 proved a tough match for early model Messerschmitt Bf 109s; but the later 109E and F models were clearly superior. Even so, the Ishaks carried on as bomber interceptors and ground-attack fighters. Eventually, as new equipment reached Soviet air units, the I-16 was put into service as a fighter trainer, a job which it did spectacularly well; for if a pilot could fly the I-16, a Yak or a MiG was a piece of piroshki!

Although still in front-service at the beginning of World War II, the I-16 was functionally obsolete. Like the Ishak shown here, many would be shot out of the sky by more advanced German planes.

Having emerged from a blizzard of exploding flak, a B-17G Flying Fortress is assailed by a German Messerschmitt Bf-109 in *Point of No Return* by Rick Ruhman. The title of the painting alludes to the terminal phase of the B-17's bomb run, when there could be no turning back or course deviations if bombing accuracy was to be achieved.

Boeing B-17 Flying Fortress

America's premier bomber of
World War II was also an
aircraft of singular beauty

BOEING B-17 FLYING FORTRESS

The newly completed Model 299 prototype as it appeared on July 16, 1935, just outside Boeing's final assembly hangar in Seattle. The plane made its public debut nine days later.

The beautiful lines of the B-17 were presaged in the design of the Boeing Model 247, which entered commercial service in 1933. Note similarities between the Model 247 and early B-17s.

In a photograph charmingly evocative of 1930s America, Y1B-17s of the 2nd Bombardment Group pass in formation above New York City. The date was February 1935, and the planes had just embarked on a long-distance endurance flight to South America.

Some aircraft appeal to individuals, others appeal to groups; few appeal to whole generations of Americans, as the magnificent B-17 does. Part of that appeal, particularly among its former crews, lies in the aircraft's rugged construction and ability to absorb punishment that saved many young lives during bombing missions against Axis targets in World War II. But the B-17 is also loved for the sheer beauty of its lines, a beauty that remains undiminished despite the passage of years and changes in aircraft technology.

The Boeing Model 299 four-engine bomber seemed destined to be a classic from the moment of its public unveiling at Boeing Field, Seattle, on July 25, 1935. With its silver fuselage glinting in the sun and its plexiglass blisters shining brightly, the big aircraft could hardly fail to impress the crowd gathered to witness the event. It had hardly rolled off the assembly line when it was dubbed "Flying Fortress"; yet for all its apparent beauty and power, the aircraft had to endure both engineering growing pains and a bitter initiation into combat before it truly earned its legendary status.

The decision to develop the Model 299 was fraught with risk for the Boeing Aircraft Company. When in 1934 the Army Air Corps announced a competition for a new multi-engine bomber, much of the design for the Model 299 had already been completed; all that remained was to build a prototype. But this would require a monetary outlay of no less than $275,000. In the present era, when a single B-2 bomber can cost upwards of $500 million, the amount Boeing committed to the Model 299 seems laughably small. It was, in fact, a huge sum for that Depression-strapped decade. (To get an idea how huge, consider that Boeing's engineers were delighted to be making seventy-five cents an hour while throwing in generous helpings of free overtime.)

The size of this expenditure warned of the very real possibility of financial ruin should the Model 299 prove a failure. But Boeing, confident that the 299 would ultimately triumph, and aware that faint heart never fortune won, went ahead with the project. In doing so Boeing

The B-17E (*top*) featured paired .50 caliber machine guns in dorsal and ventral turrets, and two .50 caliber guns in a manual turret in the tail. A distinguishing feature of the B-17F (*above*) was its single-section, molded Plexiglas nose.

Colin Kelly's Last Flight by James Dietz depicts the final moments of Kelly's B-17D, shot down off Luzon in the Philippines on December 10, 1941. Kelly was killed in the incident, and was awarded a posthumous Medal of Honor.

demonstrated that it was then (and continues to be) a conservative company in every respect save for the belief it invests in itself. On numerous occasions—the 707, 727, 737, and 747 are modern instances—it has essentially placed all of its assets on the line in the belief that a new design would see production. This willingness to gamble is now something of a Boeing tradition. But it is a tradition that started with the development of the Model 299.

The Assistant Project Engineer on the 299 Project was 24-year-old Edward C. Wells, regarded by all who knew him as a genius. (A modest man, he was the only one who would dispute the use of this term.) Wells built on the heritage of the Boeing company to meet Army Air Corps specifications, producing a truly inspired design that represented the distillation of lessons learned in designing the waspish Boeing fighters, the sleek Monomails, the revolutionary Model 247 transports, and the gigantic XB-15. The resultant Model 299 seemed to have everything going for it, especially after successfully completing its first test flight on July 28, 1935. On October 30, however, the 299 crashed in flames at

Wright Field before an audience of Army Air Corps officers who were on hand to evaluate the aircraft for military use.

The crash came very close to foreclosing on the 299's career, and the Boeing Aircraft Company as well. Fortunately for both, an investigation revealed that the crash had been caused not by any fundamental design flaw, but by human error: prior to take-off, the pilot had neglected to move the elevator control lock lever (which was located internally) to the unlocked position, thus rendering the aircraft uncontrollable in flight. In the event, such was the airplane's promise that the Army decided to place an order for 13 Y1B-17s. (If you watch the late-night movies often enough, you can see those few Y1Bs flying in perfect formation in the aviation film classic, *I Wanted Wings*.)

The Y1B-17s were used to develop long-range navigation techniques as well as to exploit the capabilities of the new super-secret Norden bombsight. Not surprisingly the results achieved by the Norden—obtained in the clear, non-hostile skies of domestic bombing ranges—were excellent. The Y1B-17 thus served to confirm

current American doctrine that fast bombers, flying in defensive formation at high altitudes, could penetrate enemy territory without a fighter escort. It was an ingenuous and brash assumption, and one that would eventually cost many lives.

One of Ed Wells' great attributes was his ability to constantly improve the basic B-17 design. A key improvement was the installation of General Electric turbo-superchargers on the Wright Cyclone engines that powered the Y1B-17As and subsequent variants. The superchargers raised the top speed from 260 miles per hour to 300 miles per hour at 30,000 feet, and literally lifted the Fortresses to a height where they could have a fighting chance against enemy fighters. If the B-17s and B-24s had not had the turbo-superchargers, they could not have operated in European skies during World War II.

Notwithstanding their potential, the United States had a mere 23 B-17s in its inventory when war broke out on September 1, 1939. And these aircraft were hardly ready to go to war, lacking as they did self-sealing fuel tanks, armor plate, and a variety of other combat necessities.

The Second World War rescued the B-17 from oblivion, for Boeing was on the verge of shutting down

Left: B-17 waist gunner at his post. Although formidable, the B-17's defensive armament was nonetheless inadequate against enemy fighters. *Above:* A claustrophobic's nightmare, the B-17's ventral ball turret was entered through a hatch during flight. Gunners had to be men of diminutive stature and high courage, since the turret's cramped confines mitigated against the wearing of a parachute.

were made to have the United States Army Air Force do the same.

But the entire American air doctrine was on the line. All of the years of planning and training, the creation of the B-17, the potential of the Norden bombsight—*everything* called for a massive American attempt at daylight precision bombing. Appointed to command America's daylight bombing campaign was Major General Ira Eaker, a brilliant airman who firmly believed that unescorted bombing raids were viable. To prove this point, Eaker began using his Eighth Air Force bombers in day probing attacks against the perimeter of the European continent in late 1942. On January 26, 1943, he dispatched 91 bombers in a raid against the naval base at Wihelmshaven, the first target in Germany to be attacked by American aircraft. Only three of the B-17s failed to return, a loss rate of 3.3 percent, which was deemed to be high but sustainable by Eighth Air Force commanders.

The pace and scale of the raids against the continent accelerated rapidly, resulting in a concomitant build-up in Eighth Air Force bomber strength. To make this build-up possible, the B-17s were supplemented by the newer, faster, yet more vulnerable Consolidated B-24 Liberators. But as the missions were extended deeper into enemy territory, German air defenses became more effective—and deadly. Soon the bomber loss rate had risen to eight percent of force totals. This innocuous-sounding statistic meant that each B-17 crew could, on average, expect to survive no more than 12 missions of its 25-mission tour. The concept of completing 25 missions—the number needed for an aircrew member to be rotated stateside—thus assumed a kind of

Ground crew load 100-pound bombs into the bay of a B-17F on a British airstrip. Although the F model had a maximum bomb load capacity of about 9,600 pounds, normal load was usually about 4,000 pounds for missions over Germany.

the bomber's production line when the conflict in Europe began. The decision to do so was quickly rescinded as orders for the aircraft came rolling in. At this stage the Boeing management, as well as American strategic bombing proponents, had good reason to believe that both the B-17 and the theories that had spurred its development would soon be put to the test.

And so they were. But initially the outcome was not as expected, much

less hoped for. In the spring of 1941 Britain received 20 B-17Cs, which were designated Fortress I by the Royal Air Force. The RAF attempted to use the Fortress Is in daylight raids, with disastrous results. More than ten of the aircraft were lost and all were plagued with mechanical problems ranging from landing gear failure to the guns freezing up. The failure of the daylight raids helped convince the RAF to stick with area bombing by night, and strong efforts

The B-17 could sustain severe damage and keep flying. With its tail all but sheared off, this B-17 returned to base after colliding with a German fighter.

Aerial Armageddons: The Schweinfurt and Regensburg Raids

History has shown us that the preparations a nation makes for war are usually incomplete. Even when war objectives are known, the technological wherewithal to achieve them may not be available. This was the case with the bombing campaign against Germany that was undertaken by America's Eighth Air Force in 1942 and 1943.

The technological problems that confronted Eighth Air Force commanders were twofold, and stemmed from their adherence to the doctrine of daylight strategic bombing. First, the application of this doctrine depended on bombers that were largely incapable of protecting themselves against fighter attack. Second, escort fighters with the range to accompany the big planes into Germany, although in production, were not yet available.

The vulnerability of the bombers of the "Mighty Eighth" was never more apparent than in the twin missions to Regensburg and Schweinfurt on August 17, 1943. Ample warning of what was in store for the Americans was provided in the weeks just prior to the raids, when the bomber loss rate had soared to 8.5 percent; nevertheless, a decision was made to conduct a coordinated strike against the two cities in what would be the deepest U.S. penetration of Germany to date.

Things went badly from the start. A low cloud cover temporarily grounded the bombers of the Schweinfurt force at their bases in southern England, thus disrupting a scheduled rendezvous with escort fighters.

While the Schweinfurt force waited for the sky to clear, Major General Curtis LeMay's Fourth Bombardment Wing proceeded to attack the Messerschmitt Bf 109 assembly works at Regensburg. LeMay's force completed its mission, then flew across the Alps and the Mediterranean to land in North Africa. Bombing accuracy had been good, but the damage to the American bomber wing had been heavy. Worse, the raid had occurred in advance of, rather than simultaneously with, the raid on Schweinfurt. That meant that German fighter strength would not be divided in their efforts to attack the incoming bomber forces. Nor would they be hindered by Allied escort fighters, mostly Republic P-47 Thunderbolts, which were forced by

Image of breathtaking horror, taken during a raid on Axis rail yards in Yugoslavia, shows a B-17 exploding in flames after it was hit by flak. More than a third of all the B-17s ever built were lost in combat.

their limited range to turn back at the German border.

The Schweinfurt raid, which was carried out by 230 Fortresses of the First Bombardment Wing, had as its objective Germany's main ball bearing production facilities. The American bombers did not reach their target until early afternoon, by which time the Regensburg force was well on its way to North Africa. The Luftwaffe was up in strength, and employed every conceivable tactic against the American bombers, from lobbing in rockets from twin-engine fighters, to dropping bombs on the formations from above, to attacks by entire fighter squadrons in a "javelin-up" formation.

Some 230 B-17s had been dispatched against Schweinfurt, while 146 were sent to Regensburg. Only 188 of the Schweinfurt group actually made it to their target; the Regensburg group fared slightly better, with 127 bombers carrying out their attacks. Although they dropped an unprecedented bomb load of 774 tons on the targets, a total of 60 heavy bombers were shot down (36 at Schweinfurt, 24 at Regensburg). This constituted a 16 percent loss rate of dispatched aircraft, and 20 percent of those attacking! And these figures did not take into account the additional 47 aircraft that had returned to base so badly damaged that they had to be scrapped.

A loss rate of 20 percent could not be sustained, for it meant that there would be a 100 percent wastage of crews and aircraft every five missions. Nevertheless, the Americans mounted a second attack against Schweinfurt on October 14. The results were similarly disastrous: out of 291 attacking B-17s, 58 were shot down while another five crash-landed in England.

Tragically for the American airmen involved, the raids in August and October were of small consequence to the Allied war effort. Although the bombs hit their targets, they did not destroy them; the German aircraft and ball-bearing factories were put out of commission only briefly, returning to full production within a few weeks.

What the raids did demonstrate was the inability of the B-17s to protect themselves, and the absolute necessity of providing them with fighter escort all the way to and from their targets. In the absence of such fighters, the Eighth Air Force drastically curtailed the long-range missions. Relief came in early 1944 in the form of the North American P-51 Mustang. The long-range Mustangs could ride herd on the bombers to Berlin and beyond. With the Mustangs fending off enemy fighters, bomber loss rates dropped significantly, and the war took a turn for the better for the brave American bomber crews.

Above: A chaplain at an English air base conducts a religious service for a B-17 crew, shortly before the latter embarked on a bombing raid against Axis-occupied Europe. The airmen had good reason to pray, given the large number of casualties sustained by the USAAF in the daylight bombing campaign. *Right:* In addition to the .50 caliber "cheek" gun on his left, the bombardier of the B-17G was armed with a pair of .50 caliber guns in a remotely operated Bendix "chin" turret. The installation of the chin turret added a whole new and effective dimension to the defensive capability of the B-17, which had previously been highly vulnerable to slashing frontal attacks by enemy fighters. *Below:* Flying Fortresses line up for take-off at a base in England. America's enormous air armada inflicted mass destruction on Germany, but the ultimate effectiveness of the strategic bombing campaign remains open to question.

mystical quality, as was recorded both in the wartime film by William Wyler titled *Memphis Belle,* and by the recent Hollywood movie of the same name.

Clearly, such losses could not be sustained indefinitely. The B-17 design accordingly underwent additional improvements intended to increase the aircraft's ability to survive combat. Eventually B-17s would be armed with as many as 13 .50 caliber machine guns; in the later-model B-17G, two of these guns would be located in a "chin" turret, which provided a measure of defense, heretofore lacking, against frontal attacks by German fighters. This defensive armament was complimented by a maximum bomb load that varied from approximately 4,200 pounds in early models, to about 9,600 pounds in later models. (Bomb loads were determined by the nature of the mission, and the range to and from the target; heavy loads naturally degraded aircraft performance and limited the distance the plane could fly.)

Better tactics also enhanced the survivability of the B-17. Major General Curtis LeMay's so-called "combat box" enabled a group of B-17s to assume a formation of such height, depth, and width that the massed firepower of their guns could be used in collective self-defense. An enemy fighter that blundered into the center of a combat box might conceivably be fired upon by dozens of guns in the B-17s flying above, below, to the front and rear, and on either side of it.

As the daylight bombing campaign grew in intensity, the Germans were forced to withdraw fighter aircraft from other battlefronts in order to concentrate in large numbers against the American bombers. On a typical unescorted mission the B-17 crews might therefore expect to encounter swarms of German fighters, flown by men who assaulted the tightly held combat boxes with tenacious courage and determination. The American airmen who found themselves so embattled were told constantly that the German response to their raids was an indicator of the trememdous damage the B-17s were inflicting on the Third Reich. They also knew that they were making a substantial contribution to the Allied

cause in places like the Eastern Front, where the reduction in German fighter strength was proving highly beneficial to the Soviet war effort. Yet this knowledge could offer scant comfort as bullets from the relentless German fighters tore into their aircraft.

Ultimately, the fate of Eaker's forces depended not on better tactics or improvements to the B-17s, but to the provision of long-range fighters capable of escorting them to and from the target. The earliest escorts—British-built Supermarine Spitfires—could accompany them only just beyond the continental coastline. Republic P-47 Thunderbolts fitted with drop tanks could escort them to Aachen on the German frontier; beyond that, however, the American bombers were on their own.

And it turned out that partial coverage was as bad as no coverage at all. The Germans, who could calculate the range of the escort fighters as well as the Americans, simply waited until the escorts departed before pouncing on the bomber formations. The B-17 was fast for its size, capable of attaining a speed of 287 miles per hour at 25,000 feet. But this was not fast enough to outrun conventional Luftwaffe fighters, much less the jet-powered fighters the Germans introduced late in the war.

The toll in shot-down B-17s continued to mount, culminating in the catastrophic raids on Schweinfurt and Regensburg (see sidebar). The introduction of long-range P-51 Mustang escort fighters in early 1944 finally reduced losses to acceptable levels. Henceforth, a greater majority of B-17s would not only get through to their targets, they would also return home.

As casualty figures went down, the effectiveness of the daylight rates climbed. Just how effective the strategic bombing campaign ultimately proved to be remains at issue. But there can be no doubt that by the end of the war the B-17s had more than demonstrated their worth. The American bombers had helped to cripple German industry, wreaked havoc on German cities and infrastructure, inflicted enormous casualties on German troop concentrations and civilian population centers, and diverted German fighters, guns, and military personnel away from theaters where they might have done the Allies considerable harm.

The cost to American forces in men and materiel was immense, however. Of the 12,731 B-17s that were built, some 4,750 of the aircraft were lost in combat. This becomes an especially sobering statistic when one

B-17Gs of the 381st Bomb Group on a training flight in England. Note that the planes lack the camouflage paint scheme typical of earlier models. Late in the war, B-17s (as well as most other American aircraft) were left unpainted to reduce the rate of fuel consumption and increase speed. The amount of paint needed to cover a B-17 was weighty enough to significantly inhibit performance.

realizes that every B-17 that went down had aboard it a crew of ten.

In addition to service in the U.S. Army Air Force, B-17s served with the U.S. Navy and Coast Guard, and the RAF. Captured Fortresses were even used by the Germans, who restored crash-landed planes for Luftwaffe service under the code-name Dornier Do 200. After the war, B-17s soldiered on in a variety of roles, particularly as pilotless target drones and air/sea rescue aircraft. In civil life they have done yeoman service dropping water and fire retardant chemicals on forest fires. Today their main role is primarily inspirational in nature; a role, it must be said, that this aircraft is singularly equipped to fulfill. Whether seen in film, or in museum exhibits or airshows, the B-17 retains the power to communicate not only the beauty of its design, but the spirit of sacrifice in which it was so often flown.

Curtiss P-40 Warhawk

Despite its flaws, this rugged fighter was
one tough customer in combat

The P-40 was based on the Curtiss P-36. The 27th Pursuit Squadron P-36 shown here is painted in water soluble camouflage for the 1939 war games.

Anyone at all acquainted with the P-40 will, when mention is made of the plane, usually think first of the shark mouth painted fighters flown by the pilots of Claire Chennault's American Volunteer Group—otherwise known as the Flying Tigers (see sidebar). That's a good image, but it sells the P-40 short, for in World War II that valiant airplane was seemingly everywhere, flown by equally valiant pilots in fair weather and foul, against the best pilots and planes the enemy could put into the air.

And the P-40 more often than not triumphed against the enemy, despite its having a design that had been obsolete since well before the outbreak of the war. Controversy always surrounded the plane, and probably always will, for a wide variety of reasons. It was originally designed for "coastal defense," a concept that exemplifies the inanity of contemporary arguments between the Army and the Navy. (The Navy insisted that Army aircraft, in keeping with the Army mission to guard the American coast, had to stay within 200 miles of the coastline; while

Main image, left: Two P-40Cs emblazoned with the distinctive shark-mouth insignia of the Flying Tigers patrol the skies over China in *Tiger Two* by Jay Ashurst. *Above:* Designed as a coastal defense fighter, the XP-40 (shown here) was obsolete well before it made its first flight.

the Navy would operate farther out on the open sea.) The P-40 was also intended for ground attack, a role in which it subsequently excelled. Yet many critics considered it to be a retrograde step in aviation design, an overweight and underpowered throwback.

The problems associated with the P-40 stemmed from its basic design, which was derived from the Curtiss Model 75—better known as the Hawk 75. Essentially, the P-40 was a Hawk 75 with a different engine. The Hawk 75 was itself the product of intense competition between American aircraft manufacturers for military contracts. The Curtiss company had for years been the primary supplier of fighters to the Army Air Corps. Curtiss had accordingly been shocked when, in 1932, the Boeing company displaced it with the P-26 "Peashooter." Determined to regain preeminence in the fighter aircraft market, Curtiss made a successful bid for the services of Donovan R. Berlin, a brilliant young engineer then in the employ of the Northrop company. Berlin was soon established at Curtiss' Buffalo plant, there to begin work on a new fighter intended to win an Army Air Corps competition scheduled for May 1935.

The fruit of Berlin's labors was the Hawk 75. In terms of structure, this beautiful, low-wing monoplane had much in common with previous Northrop designs; the retractable landing gear, however, was based on a mechanism patented by Boeing. But the Hawk 75 was underpowered, which caused the Army to balk at purchasing the aircraft. When better performance was achieved with the installation of the Pratt & Whitney Twin Wasp radial engine in 1937, the Army placed an order for 210 Hawk 75s—henceforth to be known by the designation P-36.

The P-36 had a brief and lackluster career with the Army. Export versions of the plane distinguished themselves in foreign service, however. France purchased 1,130 of the Curtiss Hawks, many of which saw combat against the Luftwaffe when the Germans invaded in May 1940. Britain also acquired a number of Hawks. The purchase of these and other American aircraft by France and Britain was immensely impor-

P-40Bs of the 33rd Squadron, 8th Pursuit Group, at their base in Langley, Virginia, in 1941. The 8th was the first air unit to be entirely equipped with the P-40.

tant to the United States, for it permitted the expansion of the American aviation industrial base at a time when there was no direct funding from the government, and little support for rearmament among the civilian populace.

The XP-40 came into being when the tenth model of the P-36 was fitted with an 1,150-horsepower Allison V-1710 in-line 12-cylinder engine. The prototype flew on October 14, 1938, and the Army subsequently placed an order for 524 of these aircraft, a huge number for the day. It was the start of a production run that would ultimately result in no fewer than 13,176 fighters being built.

France and England both purchased P-40s in large quantity, although none arrived in France before that country was defeated by Germany in June 1940. At this stage the P-40 was still not up to European standards in firepower; the P-40B had only two .50 caliber machine guns in the nose and two .30 caliber guns in the wings, while the P-40C had the same nose armament and two .30 caliber guns in each wing for a total of six guns. British fighters, by contrast, were armed with as many as eight machine guns, or a combination of eight machine guns and cannons. Performance was also deficient; the P-40's top speed of 342 miles per hour compared unfavorably with the speeds attained by the Spitfire Mk I and the Messerschmitt Bf-109E (365 and 354 miles per hour, respectively).

Instructed by the experience of war, Curtiss wrought many changes in the P-40's design, among them the addition of self-sealing fuel tanks, a heavier armament, bullet-proof windshields, and armor plate. On the plus side, these additions increased the P-40's combat effectiveness and survivability; but at the cost of added weight, which detracted from performance. To cope with this problem,

"Konkubine," a P-40 serving in the China-Burma-India theater, is armed with a 500-pound bomb. By mid-war, when this photograph was taken, it only *seemed* that every USAAF P-40 squadron had adopted some version of the AVG's shark-mouth insignia.

new and more powerful engines were also developed, with the Curtiss engineering teams adapting the basic P-40 airframe to accommodate them. Over time, the P-40's nose contours were altered, the fuselage was lengthened, and, in most instances, the overall weight was increased.

The P-40 was known by one of three names, depending on the model and the nation with which it served. The traditional "hawk" appellation was an end-component of every name, however. In RAF service, the P-40B and C were called "Tomahawk," while the D and E models were nicknamed "Kittyhawk." In American service, all versions were designated "Warhawk," although "P-40" was the term used by pilots.

The P-40 first distinguished itself in combat in the Middle East, where RAF Tomahawks and Kittyhawks became the scourge of Axis ground forces, in the process acquiring a tremendous reputation for their ability to absorb punishment. In the air the P-40s were often opposed by Italian aircraft, which were generally of inferior quality. Only the later Macchi Mc 202 proved a match for the Curtiss fighters.

By the middle of 1942 the P-40 was engaged in every major theater of war—Britain, Africa, the Soviet Union, China, Alaska, and the South and Southwest Pacific. The climates in which they fought ranged from the arctic to the sub-tropical, and everything in between. Air operations directed toward the Aleutian islands of Attu and Kiska (invaded by the Japanese in June 1942) presented the P-40 with one of its toughest weather challenges: dense, low-lying fog in the summer months, and blinding snowstorms, near-constant darkness, and sub-zero temperatures in the winter months. Yet neither the weather nor the Japanese could prevail over the robust P-40, which overcame all adversity to strike hard and often at enemy forces in the air and on the ground.

In November of 1942, P-40s were flown off aircraft carriers in support of Operation Torch—the Allied invasion of North Africa. Incredibly, none of the American P-40 pilots had ever fired their guns in anger—this was to be their first combat mission. It is a

A P-40L, headed for a base in North Africa, takes off from the carrier USS *Ranger* in March 1943. Allied P-40s operating in the Mediterranean theater excelled as ground attack planes, and were the terror of Axis transport aircraft as well.

testimony to these pilots—and to the planes they flew—that they got away from the carrier flight decks without incident, and proceeded from there to acquit themselves well in combat.

The following year, P-40s participated in the most famous episode of the air war in North Africa, the so-called "Palm Sunday Massacre" of April 18, 1943. On that date an Allied force comprising some 70 American P-40s and British Spitfires intercepted a large formation of German JU-52 transport aircraft en route from Italy to Tunisia. The Ju-52s were escorted by Axis fighters—Messerschmitt Bf 109s and Bf 110s, and Italian Macchi Mc 202s—but to no avail. Within the space of approximately ten minutes, the Allied aircraft shot down between 50 and 70 of the transports (the exact number was never determined), and 16 fighters. Six P-40s and one Spitfire were lost in the battle.

Although this action represented the nadir of Axis air operations in North Africa, it was not the end of their misfortunes. The next day the Allies shot down another 12 Ju-52s, out of a smaller formation of 20 aircraft. Then, on April 22, four squadrons of South African Air Force P-40s joined with two squadrons of Spitfires to destroy a formation of Messerschmitt Me 323 Gigants— huge motorized gliders that were

powered by six engines. The Allied fighters downed all 21 of the Gigants as well as ten fighters, thereby forcing the Luftwaffe to halt daytime supply flights to Tunisia.

The P-40E is typical of the mid-series P-40s. Powered by the Allison V-1710-39 engine, it was armed with six .50 caliber machine guns (three in each wing), and could carry up to 700 pounds of bombs, including a single 500-pounder. Top speed was 354 miles per hour, still not in the same league with its European counterparts, but superior to Japan's Mitsubishi Zero. To provide more power, a Packard-built, Rolls-Royce Merlin was installed in production P-40Fs. The 1300-horsepower engine provided a top speed of 364 miles per hour at 20,000 feet. As the demand for Merlins was great, however, subsequent P-40s reverted to the Allison engine.

By mid-1943, the P-40's days as a front line fighter were clearly numbered by new fighters then in production. The most notable of these were the Republic P-47 Thunderbolt and the North American P-51 Mustang—both of which had considerably better performance than the latest P-40. Even so, Curtiss believed there was still some stretch in the basic P-40 design, even with an airframe that was ten years old. The upshot of this belief was the P-40N,

The Flying Tigers

Romanticized in both the media and the movies, the Flying Tigers captured the imagination of the American public since the day they were formed. Their celebrity derived in part from having a jut-jawed iron ass like Claire Chennault as their commander, in part from having a popular actor like John Wayne represent the group on film (in *The Flying Tigers*). The famous sharkmouth livery that decorated the air intakes on their P-40s also did wonders for their image. But the real appeal of the Flying Tigers stemmed from the fact that they were American *volunteers* serving as courageous Davids against the Japanese Goliath.

The American Volunteer Group (the official name) was a mercenary outfit of American pilots fighting in China, under the auspices of the Chinese government, against the Japanese. The idea for the AVG (as it was also known) originated with retired Army captain Claire L. Chennault, who since 1937 had been serving as a special advisor to the Nationalist Chinese Air Force. It came into being after an intensive lobbying effort by the Chinese, acting in concert with sympathizers in America, persuaded President Roosevelt to allow for its formation. Roosevelt didn't need much persuading, despite legitimate questions about the legality of the AVG—questions that have resurfaced in recent years in the wake of the Iran-Contra affair. On April 15, 1941, he signed an executive order instructing the Army and Navy to allow the resignation of reserve pilots (without loss of seniority should they choose reinstatement) for the purpose of enlisting in the AVG.

The Army, Navy, and Marine pilots who signed on with the AVG were an eager bunch. Chennault offered them plenty of incentive: adventure, high pay, and a chance for combat. Each pilot would earn about $600 per month, plus a $500 dollar bonus for every Japanese plane they shot down. About 100 pilots and 200 ground crew eventually made the trip to China; with them went 100 obsolete Curtiss P-40Bs, which had been diverted to the AVG after having been earmarked for sale to Sweden.

The AVG was divided into three squadrons, nicknamed "Adam and Eves," "Panda Bears," and "Hell's Angels." The Adam and Eves and Panda Bears (1st and 2nd Squadrons) were originally based at Kunming,

Claire Chennault conveys something of his iron will in this photo, taken when he was a Major General commanding the 14th Air Force in China. Chennault devised tactics that enabled his obsolete P-40s to triumph over superior Japanese planes.

China; the Hell's Angels (3rd Squadron) was originally based at Rangoon, Burma. The primary mission of all three was to protect the Burma Road, China's vital supply line to the outside world. The two squadrons at Kunming first saw action on December 20, 1941, and the Rangoon squadron was blooded in combat the very next day.

Chennault was a strict disciplinarian who had thought long and hard about the conduct of air combat. He also had considerable experience at fighting the Japanese. Combining theory with experience, he developed the tactic of using two-ship fighter elements in hit-and-run attacks from above. He would not allow his American pilots to fight any other way: no individual dogfighting was permitted. This tactic played to the weakness of the more maneuverable Japanese planes, which were built of lightweight materials to enhance range, and were thus extremely vulnerable to the hard-hitting diving attacks executed by the Flying Tigers.

The AVG was disbanded on July 4, 1942. Over the course of their existence, they achieved 286 kills (with an equal number of probables) while losing only 23 aircraft in combat or accidents; and 39 of the pilots became aces with five kills or more.

After the AVG closed up shop, some of its pilots stayed on in China as

members of the 23rd Fighter Group; while others returned to air units in the service branch to which they had previously belonged. Among the best known of the latter was Pappy Boyington, a Marine pilot who personified as much as any man the fighting spirit of the unique, immortal Flying Tigers.

Colonel Robert L. Scott, seen here in his P-40 "Old Exterminator," recounted his experiences in the AVG in the best-selling *God is My Co-Pilot*.

which had an entirely new lightweight structure. The elimination of two machine guns and a reduction in fuel tank capacity brought the empty weight down to 6,000 pounds, compared to the 6,594-pound empty weight of the P-40F. The P-40N was the fastest of all the production P-40s, with a top speed of 378 miles per hour at 10,500 feet; it was also built in the greatest quantity, with 5,220 being produced.

After the P-40N, Curtiss made one last-gasp attempt to improve the plane. Bearing the designation XP-40Q, two P-40Ks and one P-40N were rebuilt with improved cooling systems of very low drag, the radiators being located in the wing. The rear of the fuselage was cut down and a bubble canopy installed, while the water-injected 1,425 horsepower Allison engine was equipped with a four-blade propeller. In one version, the XP-40Q's wings were clipped to a mere 35-feet from the original span of 37 feet, four inches. The modifications improved performance with a top speed of 422 miles per hour. But this was still less than the speeds attained by the Mustang and the Thunderbolt, and the P-40 design was retired.

In most cases the P-40 was pitted against more technically advanced adversaries; nevertheless, the plane's good flying qualities and tremendous structural integrity usually compensated for its performance and handling shortcomings. For that reason, the P-40 was generally loved by the pilots who flew it, even though they were painfully aware of its faults.

With training and experience, a skilled pilot could learn to push the P-40 to the limits of its performance, using the plane's better characteristics to cancel out its negative features. Wise P-40 pilots avoided combat above 15,000 feet (despite a nominal service ceiling of 30,000 feet), and never tried to maneuver with the enemy. Instead they employed "dive and zoom" tactics against enemy fighters, which were inevitably more nimble than the P-40. Just prior to an encounter with enemy aircraft, the P-40 pilots would seek to gain an advantage in altitude; whereupon they would make one diving pass through the enemy formation, then streak for home at full power. When

Scramble! Fighter pilots of the 14th Air Force in China sprint to their P-40N Warhawks. The photograph was probably taken in late 1943, shortly before the P-40s were replaced by P-51 Mustangs.

handled in such a manner, the P-40 could be a formidable weapon.

Ruggedly built, the P-40 could perform violent aerobatics, and would remain intact after sustaining heavy damage from enemy fire. Pilots described it as a sweet airplane to fly, although its narrow landing gear made it prone to ground looping (a sharp, uncontrollable turn on take-off or landing, causing the wingtip to

drag on the ground). The P-40 also required a strong leg on the rudder, and constant rudder adjustment.

The P-40 still takes a strong leg on the rudder, although its flying is now confined to air shows. But this is only appropriate for a plane that will always have a strong hold on the emotions of patriots who rightly see in it the full expression of World War II America.

The XP-40Q represented a final effort to update the Warhawk design. Despite improved performance it was still inferior to more modern aircraft, and thus marked the end of the venerable P-40 line.

Short Sunderland

Like its namesake, the Flying Porcupine bristled with weapons

If the Spitfire and the Hurricane won the Battle of Britain, it might be said that the Short Sunderland won the Battle of the Atlantic, suppressing the German U-boats with constant vigilance and unrelenting attacks.

These elegant flying boats, the culmination of a long line of beautiful marine aircraft, spent most of their service careers on long, tedious ocean patrols that took them through some of the worst weather in the world. A typical patrol could last from ten to 12 hours at a stretch, during which time the Sunderland crews were always on the alert for enemy submarines and vulnerable to attack from long-range German fighter aircraft. The Sunderlands combined their surveillance role with savage attacks through withering flak on U-boats and surface warships, also functioning on occasion as air-sea rescue planes.

The original firm of Short Brothers was founded in 1908 (it was called Shorts, the name persisting to this day), when it became the first British firm to acquire a license to build Wright biplanes, working with Wilbur Wright himself. Inspired by Wright designs, the Shorts were soon developing their own aircraft, producing a series that continues in the current Short commuter airliners. The Short brothers were also pioneers in lighter-than-air craft such as their reconnaissance balloons of 1907 and their Naval Airship No. 1 of 1911. The latter, nicknamed "Mayfly," never got off the ground, having collapsed while being placed in its shed. Following this failure, the Shorts built larger, more successful airships during the First World War.

Short built some excellent torpedo planes during the First World War, and immediately afterwards constructed the Silver Streak, Britain's first all-metal plane. The Short name became world famous with the pro-

duction of a series of flying boats that were used to knit the far–flung elements of the British Empire together. Most of these flying boats were biplanes powered by three or four engines slung between the wings. Beetling along at 100 miles per hour or so, the planes covered distance at an excruciatingly slow pace, and with the passing of each interminable mile their well-heeled passengers became ever more anxious to arrive at the next destination in time, presumably, for pink gins and dinner. But the airlines that operated them were happy enough with the flying boats, inasmuch as they didn't have to build runways at exotic destinations—any ocean, lake, or sizeable river would do. These lovely passenger planes reached a design pinnacle with the Empire series, four-engine, high-wing monoplanes capable of carrying 20 passengers at a top speed of 200 miles per hour.

Thus when the British Air Ministry called for a long-range general-purpose flying boat in 1933, Short was in an excellent position to provide it. The result was the inimitable Sunderland. A huge flying boat for the time, with a 112-foot wingspan and maximum gross weight (in later models) of 65,000 pounds, the clean-lined Sunderland offered good performance on the water as well as in the air. While the original contract called for only 12 aircraft, 749 were ultimately built.

Even though the majority of its patrols were uneventful, the Sunderland did serve on some of the most exciting missions of the war. Sunderlands were in on the start of both the Norwegian and the Greek campaigns (1940 and 1941, respectively), with one of the aircraft dipping down into the Yugoslav port of Kotor to evacuate King Peter II of Yugoslavia and his family. Four days later, another Sunderland rescued King George II of Greece.

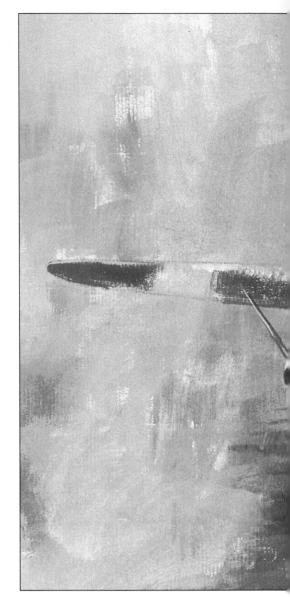

The Sunderland's armament was continually upgraded throughout the war, so much so that the Germans dubbed it the "Flying Porcupine" for the number of guns it carried. Later models were armed with up to 18 machine guns and could carry 2,000 pounds of bombs and depth charges. Radar-equipped Sunderlands became the nemesis of U-boats, surprising the submarines on the surface while the latter were charging their batteries, then sending them to the bottom with bombs, depth charges, and strafing attacks.

When Admiral Karl Doenitz, Germany's U-boat leader, reacted to the airborne threat by rearming his submarines with heavy batteries of 20 millimeter and 37 millimeter anti-aircraft cannon, the Sunderlands prosecuted their attacks in the teeth

of devastating fire. But time and again, the big flying boats demonstrated that they were tough enough to withstand a terrific amount of damage and still get the job done. Similarly, they proved remarkably capable in the many dogfights they engaged in against marauding Ju-88 fighters over the Bay of Biscay. As a counter to the German fighters, Sunderland pilots had developed a "corkscrew" maneuver that made the aircraft a difficult target to hit even as it permitted its gunners to operate their nose and tail gun turrets with maximum lethality.

The end of the war did not end the career of the Sunderland, which served in the Berlin Airlift and the Korean War. The last Sunderland on active duty served with the Royal New Zealand Air Force until 1967.

Main image, top: JU-88 Attacking A Sunderland Patrol Bomber, by W. Fritz Jurgens. Heavily armed and surprisingly agile, the Sunderland was a formidable opponent in a dogfight. *Above*: A Sunderland gathers speed for take-off.

North American F-86 Sabre

A trip down MiG Alley usually resulted in victory for this lethal beauty

Today's fighter planes are highly complex weapons systems that rely on the sophisticated technology of radars, missiles, and ground control to carry out their missions. But not the Sabre. Although equipped with some of the most advanced technology of its day, the F-86 was flown and fought the old-fashioned way, with the skill of the pilot providing the key determinant to victory. Yet that skill did not spring into

being independent of the aircraft itself. For the Sabre was one of those rare aircraft that could make decent pilots look better, and better pilots look great. Not without reason was it known as a fighter pilot's fighter plane. It was the Camel updated, the Triplane supreme, the Mustang squared; it was a joy to fly, and beautiful to behold to everyone except the MiG pilot who had the misfortune to encounter it in battle.

North American began design work on the F-86 in 1944, producing a jet-powered prototype with the designation NA-134. The aircraft had a straight wing and a rather fat fuselage with an axial-flow engine that permitted a straight passage of air from the nose intake to the tail exhaust outlet. Originally intended for the Air Force, the NA-134 was ultimately developed into the Navy's XFJ-1 Fury—the first fighter the Navy

had ordered from North American. A modified variant, the NA-140, was ordered by the USAF in June 1945.

Shortly after the end of World War II, the North American design team obtained a captured German Messerschmitt Me 262 jet fighter. The results of German wind tunnel experiments were also made available to North American. A close study of these materials revealed that sweeping the wings of the fighter would enable the achievement of higher sub-sonic speeds. An as-yet unresolved drawback to this configuration was the effect of sweepback on low-speed stability. The Messerschmitt Me 262, which had about 18 degrees of sweepback, had employed unpowered leading edge slots to mitigate the problem. (It is worth noting that the Me 262 had originally been designed without sweepback; but the heavy wing-mounted engines com-

Flying an F-86 Sabre of the 334th Squadron, 4th Fighter Interceptor Group, Major J.J. Jabara shoots down his thirteenth North Korean MiG-15 in *Tiger of MiG Alley* by Paul R. Jones. Jabara was one of the top-scoring aces of the Korean War, with 15 victories officially credited. He also scored 1.5 victories in World War II.

The wing design of the F-86 owed much to the Messerschmitt Me 262, a German jet fighter-bomber that entered service in the closing months of World War II.

An FJ-1 Fury rides the elevator to the flight deck of a U.S. aircraft carrier. Although similar to the F-86, the Fury lacked swept wings, which the Navy deemed unsuitable for carrier operations.

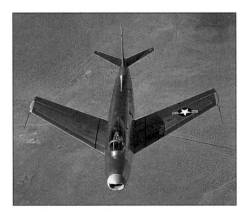

The F-86A entered squadron service in February 1949, replacing the F-80 Shooting Star. Some 554 models were built, many of which saw action in the opening stages of the Korean War.

pelled this configuration as a means of bringing the center of gravity into limits. The aerodynamic benefits were pure gravy.) However, the difficulties involved in the random operation of the 262's slots at different airspeeds and at different attitudes was unacceptable, and a new automatic slat had to be developed.

The Sabre's future was assured when Major General Bill Craigie of the USAAF, one of the great take-charge leaders in American aircraft procurement, made an on-the-spot decision to adopt a 35-degree sweep for the wings. Craigie's decision extended the development time of the XP-86, as the aircraft had been designated, but it converted what would have been a ho-hum jet into the most sensational fighter of the decade.

The Navy was somewhat concerned about operating a swept-wing fighter from a carrier deck, and opted to continue with the straight-wing variant, the FJ-1 Fury. Later, when the F-86A's tremendous performance became fully evident, the Navy cancelled 70 of the 100 FJ-1s it had ordered, and had North American create the FJ-2, a swept-wing equivalent of the F-86.

The XP-86 first flew on October 1, 1947. It was powered by an Allison J35-C-3 engine that delivered 3,750 pounds of static thrust. Equipped with a pressurized cockpit, which was placed well forward where the pilot had excellent visibility under a large bubble canopy, the XP-86 showed such promise that a budget-constrained Air Force immediately ordered 221 of the P-86As. (Note: In 1948 the letter P for Pursuit was changed to F for Fighter in Air Force designations.)

There has been a persistent—and almost certainly inaccurate—rumor that the chief engineering test pilot of North American, George Welch, actually exceeded the speed of sound in the XP-86 before Chuck Yeager accomplished this feat for the record books on October 14, 1947. While improbable, it is not impossible, for the XP-86 officially broke the sound barrier in a dive on April 26, 1948. Later, Sabre pilots would do it routinely, although the official limiting Mach number was 0.95.

North American had designed the XP-86 to assume the role previously enjoyed by their P-51 Mustang; in other words, it was to be a long-range fighter capable of imposing air superiority on the enemy at a distance. Production models of the P-86A were powered by a General Electric J47 engine that delivered 5,200 pounds of static thrust to achieve a top speed of

A wounded American pilot is helped out of the cockpit of his F-86 after tangling with North Korean aircraft in MiG Alley. Note battle damage on the fuselage just below the windscreen.

Artist Jon Balsey depicts a critical moment during a dogfight between Sabres and MiGs in *Duties of a Wingman*.

cratic neighbor to the south. At first Communist air units enjoyed an immense numerical superiority, as well as the aid of sympathizers in the South to warn of incipient American air activity. Of greater importance to Communist aircraft, however, was the sanctuary of supposedly "neutral" Red China. In fact, China actively supported North Korea, to the extent of eventually committing ground troops to the fighting; yet it maintained a facade of neutrality that was respected by United Nations forces throughout the war. The MiGs were thus able to take off unmolested from Chinese airfields, peacefully climb to altitude, and select the time of attack; after which they could land at the Chinese bases without interference.

By contrast American aircraft were forced to take off from a hodge-podge of South Korean fields and fly all the way north to the Yalu River (which constituted the frontier between China and North Korea), where they would attempt to entice the enemy into the air for combat.

This was frequently no easy task, as the enemy was not always willing to accommodate the Americans. Most of the MiGs were flown by Russian pilots who had been dispatched to Korea to receive some on-the-job training in aerial combat; and Soviet military leaders did not want their pilots to gain experience at the cost of being killed or losing their aircraft. Evidently the fate of their Communist ally was of secondary importance compared to the conservation of these valuable assets. Accordingly, and by official Soviet decree, both men and planes were often kept safely grounded.

The first MiG versus Sabre duel occurred on December 17, 1950 when a flight of F-86As from the 4th Fighter Interceptor Wing bounced four MiG-15s. In that engagement, which took place in an area that would soon become known as "MiG Alley," the first MiG kill of the war was scored by Colonel Bruce H. Hinton. It was the start of an American victory streak that would end with 729 MiGs being shot down for a loss of 78 Sabres.

The MiG-15 possessed a higher ceiling and a better rate of climb than the F-86A, which meant it could dictate when an engagement would take place. On the debit side, however, the MiG-15 was unstable at high Mach numbers, which made it seriously deficient as a gun platform. It also lacked many safety devices and redundant systems standard on the F-86. And its performance advantages were for the most part eliminated when the improved F-86E arrived in the Korean theater in October 1951. But it is less the Sabres and more the men who flew them that caused the MiG-15s to be shot down in droves. The most significant aspect of the air war in Korea, and the key to the triumph of American air power in the war, was the superior training, aggressiveness and morale of the American pilots.

All things being equal, the North Korean MiG-15 was an even match for the F-86 Sabre. But the good qualities of the MiGs were offset by the inferior skills of the men who flew them.

NORTH AMERICAN F-86 SABRE

Captain Joseph J. McConnell, Jr., became the leading ace of the Korean War by shooting down 16 MiG 15s. He scored his first victory on January 14, 1950, and became an ace within a month. On August 25, 1954, he was killed when the newly modified F-86 he was test-flying crashed in the Mojave Desert.

675 miles per hour at 2,500 feet. The P-86A had a range of 785 miles and a ceiling of 48,300 feet. Armament consisted of six 50 caliber machine guns packed in the nose—firing all six guns at once had the effect of slowing the airplane down a few miles per hour. Bombs and rockets could also be carried.

Like all classics, the F-86 underwent continuing development to incorporate the latest advances and to meet new requirements. The next new production version was the F-86E, which incorporated power boost and an artificial "feel" system. Another feature of the F-86E was the "all-flying tail"—a power-operated horizontal tail surface with the elevators linked to the stabilizer. The flying tail was derived from the lessons learned with the Bell X-1, which had used the device to ease through Mach 1.0 without loss of control. The enhanced controllability conferred by the flying tail would later prove decisive in combat with Soviet MiGs during the Korean War.

In that conflict a mere handful of Sabres, flown by what were unarguably the best-trained pilots in the world, not only kept an armada of Soviet-built jets at bay, but waxed them at every opportunity. The odds against the Sabres were fearsome: during the height of the war, the participating Communist nations— North Korea, the People's Republic of China, and the Soviet Union—had amassed more than 7,000 aircraft, of which some 1,500 were first-line fighters such as the MiG-15. In contrast, the United States averaged less than 200 Sabres at any one time in the theater (see sidebar).

The Korean War naturally caused demand for the Sabre to soar, and a second production line was opened in the former Curtiss plant in Columbus, Ohio. Reports from the so-called "MiG Alley" in Korea had indicated the requirement for greater maneuverability and more engine power. As a result the F-86F was given an uprated J47-GE-27 engine that provided almost 800 pounds more thrust. It also received what became known as the "six-three" wing. The wing's leading edge was extended six inches at the root and three inches at the tip, and the wing slat was deleted.

The F-86F first flew on March 28, 1952. Incredibly, production models equipped with an improved radar gunsight reached Korea by the fall of 1952.

The most advanced production version of the Sabre was the F-86H, which had a J73-GE-3 engine that delivered 9,300 pounds of static thrust—more than twice the thrust of the XP-86. All of the 473 F-86H Sabres that were built had their wingspan increased by two feet, and most were armed with four 20 mm M-39 cannons instead of machine guns. The cannons featured revolving drum feeds, similar to a revolver, which provided a faster rate of fire than standard machine guns.

One measure of a classic is its adaptability, and the F-86D "Sabre Dog" illustrates that quality to an amazing degree. A large, nose-mounted AN/APG-37 radar fed data into a computer system to assist the pilot in making intercepts. Instead of machine guns, the plane was armed with 24 "Mighty Mouse" 2.75-inch rockets, which were directed by a Hughes fire control system. The 700 mile-per-hour Sabre Dog was an immediate success, being *much* faster than competing two-seat interceptors, the Lockheed F-94C Starfire and the Northrop F-89 Scorpion.

The F-86 continued to be developed, and ultimately 6,203 were built for the Air Force. Some 221 F-86s were built for Italy, and a further 997 aircraft were built as FJ-variants for the Navy.

The Sabre, which was also known as the Sabre Jet, was one of those rare instances when national and military necessity, technological capability, and design aesthetics all coincided in a single aircraft. Even today, several decades after it was retired from active service, the Sabre remains unequaled in its ability to inspire respect from its opponents and affection from its pilots.

Ground crew prepares an F-86 for another mission into MiG Alley during the Korean War. Note the auxiliary wing tanks, which were dropped just before combat was joined.

A squadron of F-86F Sabres at a base in the United States. The F-86F, which was more maneuverable and possessed more engine power than earlier models, entered Korean War combat in the autumn of 1952.

The F-86D "Sabre Dog" was an all-weather variant equipped with nose-mounted radar, and armed with 24 Mighty Mouse 2.75-inch rockets instead of machine guns. Sabre Dogs entered squadron service in March 1951.

The Beechcraft Classics

Walter Beech and company produced a trio
of winners in the Staggerwing, Model 18,
and Bonanza

The Beech Aircraft Company's astonishing ability to create classics almost defies description. By producing the Staggerwing, Model 18, and Bonanza, Beech achieved what was, for the aviation industry, a feat roughly equivalent to an actor winning three Oscars in a row, or a baseball pitcher throwing three consecutive no-hitters in the World Series.

The company's first three civilian aircraft were not only classics in terms of performance and beauty; they also totally dominated the competition. Upon their respective debuts, the three aircraft were clearly superior to their rivals, so much so that each sustained its niche in the commercial aviation market over a span of decades.

This towering supremacy owed much to the leadership provided by Walter Beech. For the company's founder and namesake was one of those rare individuals who could inspire his employees to achieve their very best. As was the case with so many aviation pioneers, Walter Beech was an unlikely candidate for achieving industrial leadership; yet, like John Northrop, he was able to turn a fine intuitive engineering sense into an aircraft empire.

Beech was a farm boy whose mechanical aptitude won him a surprising degree of responsibility at an early age. Before he was 21 he repaired and installed windmills and municipal water plants; he also served as the European representative for a U.S. truck manufacturer. At 26 he enlisted in the Army Air

Main image, left: A Beech Bonanza in flight. The V-tailed Bonanza was an immediate success with the airplane flying and buying public. *Above:* Walter Beech is seen here (right) with Captain William F. Odom, who set a solo non-stop distance record in his Bonanza "Waikiki Beech."

This photograph of a restored Model 17R Staggerwing clearly shows the plane's "negative-stagger" configuration, which placed the leading edge of the bottom wing forward of the top wing.

wing was behind the cabin, with the leading edge of the bottom wing forward. (A similar arrangement had been used on the de Havilland D.H.5 fighter in World War I, and for the same reason.) The wing arrangement conferred an immediate nickname, the "Staggerwing."

Everything about the aircraft indicated quality, from the lustrous exterior finish to the retractable landing gear; yet even as the prototype was setting records, Beech was further developing the design.

By 1936, the Staggerwing was the industry's accepted standard worldwide—there was simply nothing comparable, not the Stinson Reliant, nor the Waco, nor any foreign aircraft. Its price for the time was as staggering as its wings—$18,000 and up, when a Cadillac could be purchased for $2,500.

The airplane flew—and still flies, for they are cherished classics—like a pullman car on a good roadbed; and it was fast, rock steady, and easy to maneuver. This is not to say that it was an amateur's airplane—a Staggerwing's pilot had to be proficient, especially in landing. But then, the Staggerwing had not been designed for amateurs.

The Staggerwing soon became the favorite of oil company executives, military attaches, and racing pilots. Louise Thaden and Blanche Noyes won the Bendix Trophy Race in 1936 in a Model 17, and Jackie Cochran set a new woman's speed record of 203.895 miles per hour in a special Beech D17W. Famous racing pilot Bill Ong demonstrated the strength of the

Service and became a pilot, serving as a pilot instructor. Following World War I he first worked as a designer/demonstration pilot/super-salesman for the Swallow Airplane Corporation; after which he formed his own firm, the Travel Air Manufacturing Company. His designs, initially derivatives of the Swallow, soon won most of the major races in the country, including the first two civil flights from the continental United States to Hawaii.

By 1927 Travel Air had already produced 158 aircraft, and had a backlog of 500 orders, becoming virtually the Boeing of its day. In 1929—the year of the stock market crash—it became the world's largest producer of commercial aircraft, delivering 547 aircraft and affiliating itself with the gigantic Curtiss-Wright conglomerate. It was in that year that Travel Air revolutionized air racing with the "Mystery Ship," the first civil plane to defeat military types in the National Air Races.

Walter Beech was reputed to be a daring flyer, but he was even more daring as a businessman. In April 1932, when the Great Depression was bottoming out and aircraft companies were folding like accordions, Beech and his wife, Olive Ann, formed the Beech Aircraft Company in Wichita. It was the start of a two-person team that would guide the small company from a primitive factory all the way

to the very top rung of the aviation industry. Olive Ann was at first the power behind the throne; later, during the company's greatest growth period, she became the Chairman of the Board and Chief Operating Officer.

The first Beechcraft, as Beech planes are known, was the stunning Model 17R, a five-passenger cabin biplane with a top speed of 200 miles per hour, a range of 1,000 miles, and a landing speed—critical in those days of short fields and grass runways—of only 60 miles per hour.

The Model 17R was characterized by an unusual "negative-stagger" wing layout, in which, for visibility purposes, the leading edge of the top

The prototype Model 17R as it appeared in 1932. Note that the first Staggerwing (and, for the matter, the first Beechcraft) had a fixed landing gear; production models had a retractable gear.

The prototype Model 18, seen here on a test flight in January 1937. The all–metal "Twin Beech" could carry eight passengers and crew at a top speed of 200 mph.

This artist's rendering of the Model 18 accentuates the smooth lines of the plane. A 1930s design, it resembled other, larger, aircraft of the period, such as the Boeing Model 247, the Douglas DC series, and the Lockheed twins.

Above, left: Although similar in appearance to its predecessors, the XA-38 Grizzly attack bomber was an entirely new plane, designed to carry an automatic 75mm cannon.
Above right: The Model E18S Super Twin Beech, introduced in 1954, featured an expanded cabin area with seating for ten passengers and crew.

aircraft by making daily wheels-up landings at air races in 1936 and 1937. Ong would shut off the engine, position the prop horizontally, and belly the aircraft in, sliding to a halt in less than 200 feet. Whereupon Ong's ground crew would jack the airplane up and lower the wheels, thus enabling Ong to taxi away, ready for the next day's demo.

The Second World War caused the Staggerwing to be ordered in large quantities, and production continued until 1948, when a total of 748 had been built. Today there is a Beech Staggerwing Museum, and many airshows attract beautifully restored examples of this aircraft for display.

Just as the Staggerwing was reaching the pinnacle of its civilian popularity in 1937, Beech introduced an equally revolutionary new plane, the Model 18. This was an all metal, low-wing twin engine executive airliner. Like the Model 17, the so-called "Twin Beech" was fast, handled well, had excellent structural strength, and a low landing speed.

Once again, there was simply nothing comparable in the field; the Model 18, powered by a pair of 285 horsepower Jacobs radial engines, had a top speed in excess of 200 miles per hour and a cruising speed of 190 miles per hour. Range was 1,000 miles with a pilot, copilot, and six passengers aboard.

The Twin Beech became an international favorite, serving in Canada, China, Puerto Rico (as a twin-float seaplane!), and with U.S. embassies around the world. The strength and versatility of the aircraft soon secured for Beech a series of military orders that would grow into a flood with the advent of World War II. The first to

be ordered was the F-2 photographic reconnaissance plane; there followed the AT-7, AT-11, SNB-1, C-45, JRB-10, and the all-wood AT-10 derivative. In a burst of enthusiasm, the basic Model 18 inspired the XA-38 "Grizzly" attack plane, equipped with a 75 millimeter cannon. Lack of suitable engines and changing requirements forced the cancellation of the Grizzly.

In 1969, after a record-setting 32-year production run, the last of some 7,091 Model 18s was delivered. The final version had a tricycle landing gear, which cured the tendency to ground loop displayed by earlier models equipped with tail-dragging gears—but which would make a purist Bugsmasher jockey purse his lips in disdain. ("Bugsmasher" was an affectionate nickname for the C-45, which was thought to be so slow that it could barely manage to smash the bugs it encountered in flight. The skill required to avoid ground looping the tail-dragging Bugsmasher

was a source of pride for its pilots.) Today, the Twin Beech continues to be employed in a variety of roles, including that of cargo carrier, mail plane, and passenger aircraft. And, like the Staggerwing, Model 18s also turn up frequently in the air show venue, where their restoration to wartime colors and the civilian markings of yesteryear enhance their deservedly classic status.

As World War II was grinding to a halt, Beech was in the process of developing a replacement for the Staggerwing in the post-war civilian aircraft market. Although a demand for the Staggerwing still existed, the aircraft was both technologically dated and expensive to build, having disproportionately high labor costs stemming from the time-consuming efforts required to shape and fit its many wooden parts. A new aircraft was clearly required, one as advanced and as distinctive for its time as the Staggerwing had once been.

The Rise of Civil Aviation

Civil aviation began with the Wright Flyer, and for almost 90 years it has held out the promise that tomorrow, just around the corner, private aircraft ownership might be as commonplace as owning an automobile.

It was a promise based on the notion that aircraft could fulfill the same role as the automobile, only more so. Since its advent the automobile has come to provide a tremendous degree of mobility for mankind. In the United States first, but soon in Europe, and today in third world countries, virtually everyone aspires to have an automobile. The benign hope of early aviation pioneers was that everyone would also wish to have an airplane.

But this hope has been slow to take wing. The problem is one of dimensions; not those of height and weight, but rather of direction and vector. The automobile moved in two dimensions—forward and reverse, and right or left—while the aircraft added the dangerous dimensions of *up and down*. In a car, if the engine quit, you simply pulled over to the side of the road. It was quite a different matter in the airplane.

Even though civil aviation generally withered on the vine, there were always optimistic souls who thought the future was bright, and who would capitalize on signal events like Lindbergh's 1927 flight to Paris to start up yet another company selling a peoples' plane. And there were always beautiful aircraft to beckon the customer—Pietenpol Campers, Corben Baby Aces, Eaglets, Funks, and so on.

The greatest surge came just after World War II, when it seemed inevitable that there would not only be a chicken in every pot and a car in every garage, but a light plane in every driveway as well. After all, thousands of pilots had been trained during the war, and flying had been established as a relatively safe science—so why shouldn't civil aviation boom?

And it did, for about two years. In that time some 32,000 light planes were built, many of which are still in use today. Some of these were the standard classics: Piper Cubs, Taylorcrafts, and Aeronacas. But there were some intriguing newcomers, too, such as the Ercoupe, Culver Cadet, Globe Swift, and Mooney Mite.

After 1948, however, sales plummeted, never to rise quite so high again. There have been numerous reasons

The EAA's annual "Fly-In" at Oshkosh, Wisconsin, is civil aviation's premier event.

given for this drop; they include the aforementioned three-dimension problem, the rising cost of flying, and the need to earn a living in a booming economy (flying requires a great deal of leisure time as well as money). Moreover, the physical infrastructure for private aircraft was still not developed on a scale sufficient to make flying convenient for the average man and woman. Simply put, getting around was, and is, easier for automobile owners, who have a vast road system on which to drive.

But there was another major reason, seldom mentioned, for civilian aviation's decline—the fact that flying and drinking did not mix. In the world of recreation, it was, at one time, thought reasonable to enjoy a sailboat or a motorboat—and drink. (It should be noted, however, that this attitude is now under severe fire). The fact that drinking was unacceptable with flying mitigated against its popularity.

But currently there is another surge in private flying, one that coincides with the much more sensible attitude that drinking is not necessary for a good time. Civilian aviation has been boosted by widespread public participation, and is characterized by hundreds of brilliant designs ranging from the golden oldie Fly Baby to sleek Lancairs. The movement owes its enormous vitality to the Experimental Aircraft Association, a group that was created, led, and nurtured first by Paul Poberezny, and now by his able son Tom. Based in Oshkosh, Wisconsin, the EAA has done much to foster thoughtful workmanship, innovative engineering, and the dramatic use of new materials in privately owned aircraft; and in so doing it has elevated civil flying to ever higher levels of skill, discipline, and enjoyment. Due in large measure to the efforts of the EAA, the next 30 years may well see civil aviation soar to the heights once expected of it.

The result of Beech's efforts was the Bonanza. The distinguishing feature of this beautiful aircraft was its V tail, an utterly unique configuration that replaced the conventional empennage of horizontal and vertical stabilizers (rudder and elevator) by what some called "ruddervators." Control inputs were conventional. Some pilots maintained that they could sense a "hunting" action with the V tail; that is, the tail moved slightly back and forth as if hunting for the right course, with the direction of movement occurring in the horizontal plane. But most pilots were unable to detect any performance quirks.

The new Beechcraft employed a retractable tricycle gear, and a clean, low-wing, all-metal construction; and, unlike its predecessors, it was easy to land. Public acceptance was immediate (one important reason being that it was only one-third the cost of the Staggerwing), and modern derivatives of the Bonanza remain popular to this day.

Ultimately, some 10,404 (or 10,405, depending upon which Beech record you consult) of the V-tail versions were built over an incredible 35-year production run. A version with a conventional tail debuted in 1959, and follow-on models continue to be turned out, with almost 7,000 having been produced.

The Bonanza was intended to appeal to a range of potential buyers. Accordingly, it was equipped with the kind of "options" (to borrow from automobile sales phraseology) normally not found on contemporary aircraft. Radios and advanced instrumentation came standard, thus relieving buyers of the need to procure these items from secondary sources. Hot off the assembly line, the Bonanza had the capability to carry four passengers plus baggage, and could fly under either visual or instrument flight rules. With its six-cylinder, 165-horsepower Continental engine, it could reach 184 miles per hour at sea level, and cruise at 175 mile per hour.

Like the Staggerwing and the Model 18, the Bonanza lent itself to breaking aviation records. Bill Odom made the longest non-stop solo fight in history in 1948, when he flew his Bonanza 4,957 miles from Honolulu,

Above: Bill Odom stands on the wing of his Bonanza "Waikiki Beeech" shortly before taking off on a record-setting solo flight from Hawaii to New Jersey in 1948.

Hawaii, to Teterboro, New Jersey. Ten years later, Pat Boling would up the record to 7,090 miles, in a solo flight from Manila to Pendleton, Oregon.

In 1948, a military training derivative of the Bonanza was introduced; known as the T-34 Mentor, this aircraft was just a warm-up to the deluge of ever more sophisticated multi-engine planes that would eventually pour from the Beech's Wichita assembly lines. The first Twin Bonanza appeared in November 1949, and there followed one multi-engine success after another—Travel Airs, Barons, Queen Airs, and King Airs—while at the same time, Beech's military business continued to expand.

Now the aviation world is watching to see if the latest Beech innovation, the radical Starship, will achieve the same degree of success as its predecessors. Derived from an original design by Burt Rutan, the all-composite Starship has the beauty to be a classic, as well as the engineering innovations. The Starship has three tough acts to follow—the Staggerwing, the Model 18, and the Bonanza—but if Beech is running true to form, we may assume that its classic status is virtually a foregone conclusion.

The radical Starship gives every indication of becoming the next Beechcraft to be hailed as a classic.

Above: The V-tailed Bonanza was succeeded by a conventional single-tail version, first introduced in 1959. To date some 7,000 single-tail Bonanzas like the A36 (shown here) have been built.

Bell Model 47 Helicopter

This unconventional aircraft was, fittingly, the product of two very unconventional men

Above: The durable Model 47-G and its military version, designated H-13G (shown here), was in production from 1953 to 1974, and remained in service long after the later date. *Right*: Germany's Flettner Fl 282 Kolibri was the first helicopter to be ordered into mass production. *Far right*: Bell test pilot Floyd Carlson waves from the cockpit of the Model 30, affectionaly known as "Genevieve."

The road leading to the creation of the Bell Model 47 helicopter was a long and difficult one, extending back into history, and studded with the ambitious attempts of pioneers from many countries. The road *from* the Model 47 was filled with one triumphant design after another, so that in designating this helicopter as a classic, one also honors a whole family of helicopters.

The Model 47, which was the first helicopter to receive commercial certification, was the product of two men who had little in common other than genius. Larry Bell and Arthur Young were from totally distinct walks of life, and they marched to different drummers; yet when the time was ripe, they meshed their unorthodox styles in seamless fashion to achieve success.

They had a long tradition on which to draw. In centuries past the possibility of vertical flight had engaged the intellects of some of history's greatest thinkers. Most of the early inventors experimented with models rather than full-scale aircraft, using powerplants that ranged from rubber bands to engines using black powder as the motive force. All were stymied by the same apparently insoluble problems. These involved the need to develop an engine that was lightweight yet powerful, and a lifting apparatus that was similarly lightweight, yet strong enough to withstand the forces generated by a helicopter's whirling blades. Most vexing, however, was the problem of controlling those forces.

Of the two men who collaborated on the Bell Model 47, Larry Bell is the more famous. He was of the old school of aviation pioneers, a man who experienced first-hand the rough and tumble of exhibit flying life. Later he joined Glenn Martin in Cleveland, Ohio, where he worked to create the Martin bomber series. During his tenure with Martin, Bell was in charge of purchasing, the work force, scheduling, and production. Yet, he still found time to involve himself in aircraft design. It was a hodgepodge of experience that would later induce Rueven Fleet to hire him to work for Consolidated in Buffalo, New York. When Consolidated left Buffalo in 1935 to resettle in San Diego, Bell stayed

behind to start up his own company in July of that same year.

Larry Bell's company caught the wave of prosperity brought on by the Second World War, and his factory turned out P-39 Airacobra and P-63 Kingcobra fighters by the thousands. Later, of course, his company would produce the first American jet fighter, the Bell XP-59, and the first aircraft to achieve supersonic speed in level flight, the Bell XS-1.

Arthur Young, on the other hand, was no entrepreneur but rather an unusual combination of philosopher and tinkerer. Prior to hooking up with Bell, he had embarked on the age-old quest for vertical flight as a means to discipline his intellect in the pursuit of self-eduction; and since he expected the invention of the helicopter to reinforce his understanding of philosophy and life, he was prepared to spend years at the task.

Young began his effort in 1928, drawing inspiration from the work of a German designer/engineer named Anton Flettner. (During the 1930s it was scarcely possible to pick up a copy of *Popular Science* without coming across an article about yet another of Flettner's inventions.) Flettner was attracted to the idea of employing revolving cylinders to generate

lift, and he suggested application after application for such devices, most of which proved impractical. During World War II, Flettner achieved considerable success with his own helicopters, which used rotor blades rather than rolling cylinders. The Flettner Fl 282 Kolibri (Hummingbird) entered operational service in 1943; but the Allied bombing campaign kept them out of mass production, which had been planned for 1944.

For the next *ten years,* Young applied himself patiently to building model helicopters, tackling the problems of lift, stability, and auto-rotation sequentially. Eventually he produced a model that had a stabilizer bar linked directly to the rotor, so that the rotor plane was independent of the rotor mast. The models were electrically powered, and Young taught himself to fly helicopters in the safest possible manner—standing on the ground with a control box in his hand.

In September 1941, Young made a presentation to Larry Bell and his executives, showing them a film that documented both his failures and his success. This was followed by a flying demonstration with his model, and Bell, the super salesman, was

Near the end of World War II Larry Bell (*left*), aware that the military aircraft market was about to collapse, placed an increasing emphasis on helicopter development. The helicopter pictured here is one of his early efforts.

BELL MODEL 47-G HELICOPTER

The medevac version of the H-13 helped revolutionize battlefield medical procedures. As demonstrated by this Korean War photo, a wounded soldier could often expect swift evacuation to a nearby Mobile Army Surgical Hospital (MASH).

sold. Young was hired to develop the helicopter.

Unfortunately, he joined the company just as the onset of World War II had generated a flood of aircraft orders. Helicopter development was put on the farthest burner to the rear. Nevertheless, a quarter of a million dollars was allocated to the helicopter project. Young was delighted by the amount, which he deemed sufficient to build two full-scale prototypes. But Young's delight quickly faded when he discovered that the $250,000 was for the *drawings* only, and that there were no funds available for prototype construction.

The fact that everyone was busy and his project was small ultimately worked in Young's favor, however. Young kept at the job, unnoticed and uninterrupted by his superiors. Through personal persistence, and by what today would be termed schmoozing, he managed to secure the necessary funding. But just before construction was scheduled to begin (without benefit of drawings, it should be noted), the funds were withheld. It seems that Larry Bell was concerned about what would happen to a helicopter if an engine quit—after all, such an aircraft had no wings with which to glide to a safe landing. Young arranged a demonstration for Bell. He carefully bal-

anced a raw egg in a remotely controlled model, flew the model to the ceiling of the factory, and cut the power. The little model autorotated gently down, the egg didn't break, and Bell ordered the release of funds for the project.

Never having built a full-sized aircraft, Young decided to simply scale everything up by a factor of six. Just one year later his empirical approach to helicopter design produced the Bell Model 47. Called "Genevieve" by Young and his colleagues, the Model 30 flew well except for some unexpected stability problems.

Young and his crew continued developing the helicopter as the war entered its final months. Aware that the end of the war would also bring an end to contracts for more fighter planes, Larry Bell's interest in the helicopter project increased. Mindful of the helicopter's commercial potential, Bell accordingly elevated the development of the aircraft to top-priority status.

Although not a pilot, Young himself conducted many of the tethered test flights on the Model 30. But it was veteran test pilot Bob Stanley who attempted the first untethered ride on the fractious helicopter horse—and was promptly thrown. Stanley got behind on the controls, the helicopter began to buck, and he

was tossed up into the rotor blades—which slung him out into the snow. Although the Model 30 was badly damaged, Stanley escaped serious injury to his body, if not his pride.

The Model 30 was rapidly developed into the Bell Model 47, which received its commercial certification on March 8, 1946. The Model 47 was offered for sale at $25,000, or $21,500 to dealers. By the spring of 1950, however, only about 200 had been sold, and interest in the aircraft seemed to be waning. Then came the Korean War, and an order for 500 H-13s, the military version of the Model 47. This put Bell back into the forefront of the helicopter business. The H-13s made history with their medevac work, and were later immortalized for the public in the opening scenes of the television series *M*A*S*H*.

The success of the Model 47 and all of its derivatives stemmed from the basic simplicity of the aircraft, which was in turn the result of the rather basic nature of Arthur Young's experimentation. With his limited resources, he always had to strive for the non-complex solution. His use of a two-blade, wide-chord rotor, hinged at the center so that it would "see-saw" around the mast, was complemented by a bar, also hinged to the rotor axis, which was gyroscopically stabilized by counterweights on its tips. These were connected to the cyclic control mechanism, which operated to tilt the two blades in relation to the vertical axis. Complicated in the telling, it was a far simpler system than other helicopter designers had devised.

For over 40 years Bell has been well served by the Model 47's basic layout and mechanics, which are evident in the current lines of turbine-powered HueyCobras and civil transports. The Model 47 itself has undergone continual improvements throughout the course of its long career, particularly through the addition of newer and more powerful engines. Variants have been built in quantity under license by Augusta in Italy, and by Westland in Britain. The Bell helicopters, which have functioned in a variety of civilian roles, have also served in most of the military and police forces of nations allied with the United States.

McDonnell Douglas
F-4 Phantom

One of the ugliest fighters in history also proved one of the most fearsome in combat

MCDONNELL DOUGLAS F-4 PHANTOM

Above: A look at the pilot's seat in an F-4. *Previous page*: On May 22, 1967, Phantom pilot Col. Robert F. Titus (USAF) shot down two North Vietnamese MiG-21 "Fishbeds" with a combination of Sidewinder missiles and cannon fire. In *Titus Gets His First*, artist Lou Drendel shows the first MiG plummeting earthward in flames, while the second MiG attempts to flee moments before it, too, falls victim to the pursuing American plane.

An F-4 Phantom with the Missouri National Guard zooms for altitude. The shark-mouth motif, popularized by the Flying Tigers of World War II fame, remains a favorite of American aircrews.

According to an old aviation cliche, "If it looks good it'll fly good." While that may often be true, good looks don't always tell the tale. The McDonnell Douglas F-4 Phantom is a case in point. The aircraft's official nickname was "Phantom II," but in popular parlance it was called "Old Double Ugly" or "Rhino" because of its unconventionally angular appearance.

Despite its unaesthetic features, the F-4 is one of the all-time classic fighter aircraft. First flown on May 27, 1958, the Phantom has since proved its combat worth in countless battles, the most recent occurring in the 1991 Persian Gulf War, where the F4-G Wild Weasel and reconnaissance RF-4s were absolutely indispensable. So excellent was the Phantom's performance in the war that plans to retire it from active service were subsequently shelved.

The Phantom had its start in a relatively modest proposal from the McDonnell Aircraft Company to the U.S. Navy in 1953. While no requirement existed for such an aircraft, McDonnell proposed building an all-weather, long-range, single-seat fighter, essentially an upscale version of their previous aircraft, the F3H Demon. The basis of the proposal was that by using seven different, interchangeable nose sections, the new fighter could perform a wide variety of missions. This meant that an aircraft carrier could field just one

type of aircraft for most of its duties, with tremendous resultant savings in spare parts, training, and other potentially expensive areas.

Although the Navy was not especially responsive to the proposal, McDonnell persisted, each time garnering new ideas as to what might sell. What eventually emerged after five years of reciprocal negotiations was a twin engine, two-seat aircraft powered by General Electric J79 engines, and equipped with missiles only—no guns. The emphasis on the aircraft's configuration as a *two-seater* is important, and will be discussed below.

During this period in the late 1950s the unconventional aspects of the Phantom's appearance slowly emerged. After wind tunnel tests showed that the Mach 2 fighter would encounter severe stability problems, the aircraft's design was steadily altered. The once-flat wing was given 12 degrees dihedral on the folding outer wing panels, and the leading edge was shaped into a "dog-tooth" form. The tailplane was drooped to have 23 degrees anhedral, and a necessary fine-tuning of the variable geometry air intakes was performed. When all the tweaking was done, the rather handsome design of the original had been transformed into "Double Ugly."

"Mr. Mac," better known as James Smith McDonnell, Sr., the founder of McDonnell Aircraft, was pleased

with the F-4 and he was further pleased by the Navy's order for 376 of the fighters. But sales of the F-4 did not end with the Navy. To everyone's amazement, demand for the aircraft grew almost daily, spreading first to the Air Force and then around the world to countries allied with the United States. To meet the demand, some 5,201 F-4s were eventually produced, a record for Western jet fighters that will probably never be exceeded.

Although the Phantom's wingspan was just over 38 feet, it was nonetheless a *big* aircraft. The F-4E variant was 63 feet long and had a maximum weight of 61,795 pounds, more than a fully loaded B-17F of Second World War vintage. Yet from the very start its performance was exceptional, as was demonstrated when it set records for speed (1,606.3 miles per hour, almost Mach 2.6), absolute altitude (over 100,000 feet), sustained altitude (66,237.8 feet), climb rate (many different records, but 114.5 seconds to 15,000 meters), and transcontinental flight (two hours and 48 minutes.)

The Phantom's blistering performance resulted in an amazing mission adaptability. With nine stations for stores, the F-4 could carry an enormous load of munitions, fuel tanks, electronic countermeasures gear, and nuclear weapons. The principal armament was originally intended to be Sparrow III air-to-air missiles, supplemented by Sidewinder missiles. Subsequent additions to the list included the rocket-assisted GBU-15 glide bomb, and a wide variety of air-to-ground missiles such as the Shrike, Maverick, and Standard ARM and HARM. An entire array of "dumb, smart, and brilliant" bombs could also be carried. Early variants such as the Navy F-4B and the Air Force F-4C were fitted with external gun pods, but the pod-mounted guns were not a success, being both inaccurate and detrimental to aircraft performance.

The Phantom proved to be an easy plane to fly—as long as it was kept well within the limits of its defined performance elements. When flown at heavy weights, through the wild maneuvers necessary to avoid enemy antiaircraft gunfire and surface-to-air missiles, the Phantom was subject to "departing"; that is, passing from stable flight into a stalled flat-spin from which ejection was the only solution. Almost 200 Phantoms were lost to the departure phenomenon, and McDonnell set up a $100 million program called "Agile Eagle" to correct it by manufacturing a new wing with leading-edge slats.

The Phantom was a complex aircraft, requiring a "GIB" (guy-in-the-back seat) to manage its sophisticated weapons systems and electronic

The camera caught this Navy F-4 in the instant it was catapulted off the flight deck of the USS *Saratoga*. Another F-4 (*right*) is being readied for take-off.

countermeasures systems. The Air Force initially used pilots in that position, only to discover that this practice was a waste of trained pilots. It was also hard on the morale of the pilot-GIBs, who regarded the back seat assignment as a reduction in status. In time, Weapons Systems Officers—"Wizzos"—were specially trained to handle the back-seater duties. Still, the status problem didn't go away, particularly when an F-4 scored a kill.

By way of background, two-seat fighters have been around for many decades. Captain Andrew Edward McKeever shot down 30 German planes in his two-seat fighter during World War I, while his observer, Sergeant L. F. Powell, accounted for eight more on his own. During World War II, night fighters on both sides scored victories with multi-person crews, but it was the pilot who was credited with the kill.

This situation changed during the Vietnam War. By then, the back-seaters were no longer permanently relegated to non-command positions; and they knew that, in the race for command-level promotions, combat victories would count. Quite naturally, and in the interests of career advancement, they wanted to receive credit for the enemy aircraft they helped shoot down. Therefore the Air Force Chief of Staff, General John J. Ryan, made a decision that an F-4 pilot and his back-seater would each receive full credit for any and every plane they managed to shoot down.

As one may expect, the pilots didn't like the idea, for the distinct possibility loomed that an observer, flying with a series of different pilots scoring kills, could become the leading ace! And this is in fact what happened with Captain

James Smith McDonnell, founder of McDonnell Aircraft, poses in front of the 5,000th Phantom to roll off the assembly line. Some 5,195 F-4's were built before production ceased.

Above: Partners, a watercolor by Stephen D. McElroy, depicts a scene from the Vietnam War: Three Phantoms roar off on their next mission while an American tank crewman waves them on. *Right*: A Navy F-4B releases its bombs against an enemy position in the jungle of South Vietnam. Originally intended to serve as carrier-borne bomber interceptors, Phantoms were devastatingly employed in the ground attack role as well. However, unrealistic rules of engagement hampered their effectiveness.

Artist William S. Phillips stunningly portrayed the Phantom's speed and brutish power in his painting, *Hot In the Canyon*.

Charles DeBellevue, who scored five victories as the Wizzo with Captain Steve Ritchie, and then a sixth with Ritchie's buddy, Captain John Madden.

Anomalies like this one were bothersome to many, but the entire Vietnam War was unsettling to American fighter pilots for a variety of reasons. First, and foremost, were the restrictions imposed by the American formulated rules of engagement. At the very least, these rules severely hobbled the capabilities of the F-4 crews. Certainly, the rules did not allow the crews to take full advantage of their splendid aircraft. They were not allowed to strike at enemy airfields, nor could they engage enemy aircraft unless the latter had shown "hostile intent"; which is to say, unless their foe had commenced an attack.

Even worse, enemy surface-to-air missile (SAM) sites were not to be attacked until the sites were ready to fire. This led to absurd situations in which North Vietnamese forces could prepare a SAM site for action without interference from American crews, who were well aware of the nature of the enemy activity and the threat it portended. The Americans were further enjoined from attacking schools and hospitals even when it was known that these facilities were being used as antiaircraft gun emplacements or ammunition storage depots.

This prohibition at least had some rationale, in that it denied an obvious propaganda coup to the enemy, while providing insurance against accidental attacks on buildings that were actually in civilian use. What made no sense at all to the Americans were the orders forbidding them to attack the dikes along agricultural fields, which often bristled with antiaircraft weaponry.

Another problem confronting F-4 crews were deficiencies with regard to the aircraft's armament. While air-to-air missiles were fine for the bomber interception role, they had many shortcomings for fighter versus fighter combat, particularly when operating under the constraints imposed by the aforementioned rules of engagement. That the F-4 crews were forbidden to fire unless they had positive identification of the enemy aircraft may sound reason-

Steve Ritchie: Vietnam War Ace

Steve Ritchie is a personal friend of this writer, and I'm sure he'll forgive me if I first simply catalog some facts about him—facts which speak for themselves:

- Halfback for the Air Force Academy, playing in 1963 Gator Bowl.
- Number one in his pilot training class.
- One of the youngest instructors ever in Red Flag, the Air Force's equivalent to Top Gun.
- Served two tours in Vietnam, with 339 missions flown and over 800 hours combat.
- Holds the Air Force Cross, four Silver Stars, ten Distinguished Flying Crosses and 25 Air Medals.
- First USAF Ace in Vietnam; the *only* USAF pilot ace; and the *only* "all MiG-21" ace.

In many ways Steve is the image of the American fighter pilot—rugged good looks, quick smile, and an aggressive nature when it comes to battle. Few pilots were ever as well prepared for combat as he was, and fewer still were smart and lucky enough to have his combination of experience, training, and hot desire to get the maximum out of their aircraft.

Steve Ritchie went to Southeast Asia for the first time in 1968. He flew 195 missions, of which 95 were hazardous Stormy Fast FAC (Forward Air Controller) missions that he helped develop. FAC missions usually operated with small, slow aircraft like the North American OV-10 Bronco. Fast FAC missions were an innovation, using high speed aircraft like the F-100 and F-4 to undertake long-range tactical reconnaissance, and to facilitate planning for strikes against mobile targets.

At the conclusion of his tour, Ritchie went to the Fighter Weapons School at Las Vegas to serve as an instructor, and to translate what he'd learned into new tactics. As soon as he was eligible, he returned to the war for another tour, this time with the Triple Nickel outfit, the 555th Tactical Fighter Squadron, stationed at Ubon, Thailand.

On May 10, 1972, Ritchie and his Wizzo, Chuck DeBellevue, engaged four MiG-21s in a complex battle, downing one of the latter for their first victory. They got another on May 31,

and then on July 8 they got a double kill while inbound to Hanoi. The fifth kill came on August 28 while Ritchie was leading a MIGCAP force for a strike on the infamous Thai Nguyen steel mill.

Notwithstanding these achievements, Ritchie rendered his greatest service to the USAF upon his return from Southeast Asia, when he became an ardent proponent of rigorous, realistic pilot training, and an adviser on the characteristics to be sought in the new fighter aircraft under development. This puts him in the unique position of having fostered the good qualities of the F-15, F-16, and F/A-18 fighters used in the Persian Gulf war, and the skills of the pilots who flew them.

An elated Steve Ritchie climbs out of his F-4 at Udorn Royal Thai Air Base after shooting down his fifth MiG-21 on August 28, 1972.

Afterburners aglow, an F-4 streaks past its latest kill, a North Vietnamese MiG-21 Fishbed. With superbly skilled pilots like Steve Ritchie at the controls, Phantoms were able to score 146 aerial victories in the course of the war.

A flight of brightly painted Phantoms belonging to Navy test squadron VX-4. The orange plane is a QF-4B drone, although in this instance it is piloted.

able; but given closing speeds of up to 1,500 miles per hour, by the time identification was possible the F-4 was too near to its adversary for the crews to use their Sparrows effectively. This gave the advantage to enemy MiG pilots, who could close and use their cannons against the F-4s.

The TISEO (Target Identification System Electro-Optical) helped resolve the problem by introducing a high-resolution, long-range, closed circuit television set into the F-4. The TV image gave the F-4 crews the capability of identifying MiG-21s as far as ten miles out, and with it the freedom to use air-to-air missiles against them.

This boosted effectiveness and cheered morale, but the really significant improvement, one that was of immense satisfaction to the F-4 pilots, was the fitting of an internal gun to the F-4Es then coming off the line. This weapon, the 20 millimeter M-61 Gatling gun, was stuffed in the Phantom's nose along with a 640-round ammunition container. Although the add-on caused a number of other problems that had to be solved, it did provide F-4 aircrews with a dogfighting kill capability.

Like the Germans in World War I, the North Vietnamese air force let the customer come to the door before fighting him. It was a wise, economical policy that allowed the North

Vietnamese to send their MiGs up to engage only under the most favorable circumstances. If North Vietnamese pilots found themselves at any disadvantage whatsoever, they would break off their attack. Air-to-air combat was therefore an infrequent occurrence, as was the incidence of aerial kills. Small wonder, then, that the Vietnam War produced only five aces. Of those five, two were pilots (Ritchie and Lieutenant

Randy Cunningham, USN, now a U.S. Congressman) and three were back-seaters (Weapon Systems Officers DeBellevue and Captain Jeff Feinstein, and Radar Intercept Officer Lieutenant Willy Driscoll, USN.)

There were other reasons for the dearth of American aces. The U.S. pilots were rotated through their missions in order to spread combat experience widely throughout their respective service branches, a practice that inevitably limited victory totals. Another, less palatable explanation lies in the fact that, in engagements with American planes, the North Vietnamese optimized the characteristics of their aircraft, their ground control, and their tactics.

Finally, the low victory totals were attributable, at least in part, to the insufficiently realistic combat training that Phantom aircrew had previously undergone. To remedy this, new advanced-training flight schools were established. Known as Top Gun in the Navy and Red Flag in the Air Force, these schools are exceptionally rigorous in preparing aircrew for fighter versus fighter combat, and for that reason deserve much of the credit for the consistently outstanding performance of American fliers in the Gulf War.

Regardless of the limitations placed upon F-4 crews during the Vietnam War, the Phantom was

An F-4 sets up for a carrier landing. Seen from altitude, the flight deck seems an improbably small platform from which to operate a big plane like the Phantom.

Armed with radar-busting missiles, an F-4G Wild Weasel skims across the desert cloud cover during Operation Desert Storm. The Wild Weasel was developed solely for the purpose of destroying enemy radar installations.

indisputably a superior aircraft. As such, it was an invaluable component of U.S. armed forces in Vietnam. But it was in Israeli service that the F-4 proved vital to the survival of an entire nation and its people.

The Israelis received their first F-4s on September 7, 1969, at a time when the so-called War of Attrition was building to new heights. This conflict had begun in the autumn of 1967 when an Egyptian-led coalition of Arab states, undaunted by their crushing defeat during the Six Day War in June, embarked on a strategy of bleeding Israel dry through attritional warfare. The Egyptian (and Arab) aim was to drive Israel from the Sinai, and it was in the region of the Sinai-Egyptian frontier, as then defined by the Suez Canal, that most of the fighting occurred. The war was prosecuted by both sides with ferocious artillery barrages, skirmishes between infantry and armored forces, commando raids, and air strikes. In

May of 1969 Egyptian president Jamal Abdel-Nasser announced that a new phase in the war had started, one that would see the liberation of the Sinai; but he had not reckoned with the arrival of the Israeli F-4s, which would shortly play a huge role in thwarting his ambitions.

The Phantoms entered Israeli service none too soon for the fortunes of the Jewish state. Israel's long-time supplier, France, had suddenly and mysteriously placed an embargo on arms delivery; and having thus been denied the purchase of French aircraft, the Israelis were able to put fewer and fewer planes into the air. The Phantoms were subsequently parceled out only to the most skilled Israeli pilots (who were very skilled indeed), and were used to range far beyond Israel's borders to strike at targets deep in Egypt. When in the summer of 1970 a cease-fire ended the War of Attrition, the Israeli Phantoms had achieved an astound-

ing *25 to 1* victory ratio over their Arab counterparts. Offsetting this figure, however, were heavy losses sustained by the Israeli Phantoms to enemy SAM missiles.

The Phantom's versatility was further demonstrated in the RF-4 reconnaissance versions and the Wild Weasels. All told, the F-4 became the premier fighter of the free world, serving with ten countries, some of whom were occasionally close to war with each other. In addition, both Britain and Japan manufactured their own versions of the F-4, adapting it to their national needs.

Now, more than 30 years after its first flight, there is talk of modifying existing Phantoms with new engines and electronic systems so that they can continue to fly into the 21st century. If so, any future conflict involving the United States will no doubt see an F-4 variant adding yet more honors to an already uniquely impressive combat record.

Pioneering Jet Airliners

Postwar public demand for speedy air travel was satisfied by groundbreaking jet airliners named Comet, 707, and Caravelle.

At the close of World War II, a trio of diverse factors existed that would combine in just a few years to create the worldwide boom in commercial jet transportation.

The first of these factors was the international network of runways, radio facilities, meteorology networks, fuel farms, and other elements of a vast flight support system that had been created during the war. The second was the release to civilian occupations of a huge number of engineers who had been in the forefront of military technology, and who were conversant with jet engines and modern aerodynamics. The third factor was the realization by airline planners that a jet transport would have four or five times the productive capability of the most modern piston-engine airliner of the postwar period. Suddenly, jet transports made sense. Yet as ambitious as these planners were, none could have imagined the tremendous changes that would occur from the creation of such stellar classics as the de Havilland D.H. 106 Comet, the Boeing 707, and the Sud-Aviation Caravelle.

It is perhaps reasonable that Britain, where the jet engine was invented, should have been first off the mark. Planning at de Havilland for the Comet actually began with the authorization of design studies by the British government in March 1943, more than two years before the Axis powers were subdued. The idea of a jet transport evolved quickly from small, short-range designs carrying 20 passengers to the lovely D.H. 106 Comet, which took form in 1946 and first flew on July 24, 1947.

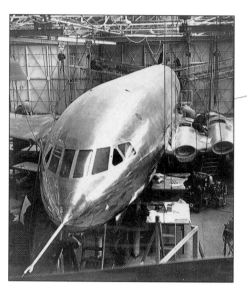

Even while under construction, the Comet had a futuristic look that seemed altogether appropriate for the world's first jet airliner.

It was a stunningly beautiful aircraft, from its sleek, somewhat drooped nose, to the elegant wings that housed four de Havilland Ghost turbojet engines. More significantly, the de Havilland firm had done an enormous amount of test work that included simulation of the temperatures and pressures that would be encountered at 70,000 feet, far above the Comet's usual 40,000-foot ceiling. The fuselage was pressure-tested to double the required pressure for cruising at altitude, a benchmark far beyond any Air Ministry requirements.

After extensive testing, the Comet entered passenger service with BOAC (British Overseas Airways Corporation) on May 2, 1952. The plane was capable of carrying 36 passengers for 1,500 miles at 500 miles per hour—200 miles per hour faster than any contemporary piston-engine airliner. The Comet was perfect for British passengers and the often-traveled routes to Rome, Beirut, Khartoum, Entebbe, Livingstone, and Johannesburg.

Passengers loved the airplane for its smoothness, comfort, and pleasing swiftness. Pilots liked flying it, although there were some handling difficulties on take-off and landing. All told, the Comet was an immediate success, setting records on each new route as it was introduced, and being sought by many foreign airlines. Best of all, it was extremely reliable, meeting schedules with a regularity no piston-engine airliner could match.

Yet there were dark threads in this silver cloud of speed and beauty, for three Comets had been lost running off the end of runways, and one had broken up near Calcutta under mysterious circumstances in a tropical rainstorm. But that wasn't the end of it; worse travail was to follow.

On January 10, 1953 a London-bound Comet broke up after take-off from Rome. The accident jolted the entire aviation world, yet so great was the general confidence in the plane's design that it was assumed that sabotage must have been the cause of the mishap. Despite extensive salvage efforts, it had not been possible to recover the wreckage to determine the reason for the crash. All the other Comets were inspected, no flaws were found, and service resumed.

Then, on April 8, 1954, a Comet

Above: John Batchelor's painting depicts a Pan American Boeing 707 in flight. Not the first jet airliner to enter service, the 707 would prove one of the most successful.

disappeared off the coast of Sicily, near Stromboli. As an intense salvage effort began, Comets were grounded worldwide.

The plane was recovered. Intensive study of the wreckage revealed that the Comet cabin had blown open as a result of metal fatigue from repeated cycles of pressurization. A failure had occurred starting at a crack in a cutout that housed the ADF antenna; under pressure the crack had spread, resulting in an explosive decompression of the cabin and the complete destruction of the aircraft.

In an instant, Britain's lead in the race for dominance in the jet age was lost, never to be regained. De Havilland did more testing and brought out the Comet 3 and 4, and one of the latter inaugurated jet transatlantic service on October 4, 1958. But the damage had been done, and new and better competitors were on the horizon.

Preeminent among these was the brilliant Boeing 707, the most important jet transport of all time. Boeing had a great advantage over any competitor, having garnered practical jet experience with the B-47 and B-52 bombers. Boeing management felt that the Air Force would ultimately require a jet tanker, and decided to take a $16,000,000 gamble in developing a prototype that could also be used as a basis for a jet transport. The new aircraft, given the spurious code designation 367-80, clearly forecast a revolution in air transportation.

Like the B-47, the 707 had a 35-degree swept wing, with four Pratt & Whitney JT3 turbojets slung under it in nacelles. The new aircraft made its

Above: Passengers in London board a BOAC Comet 4 for the first transatlantic commercial jet airliner flight on October 4, 1958. That same day, another Comet flew the Atlantic from New York City to London.

Left: The graceful lines of the Comet are evident in this John Batchelor painting. For all its beauty, however, the original Comet was a tragically ill-fated plane. Serious flaws in the Comet's design led to a series of disasters that caused the public to lose faith in the plane, and Britain to lose its dominant position in commercial jet airliner development.

Boeing test pilot A.M. "Tex" Johnston stands in the cockpit of the 707 prototype. Despite excellent performance, the 707 got off to a slow sales start in a market glutted by propeller-driven aircraft.

The KC-135A tanker was a military variant of the 707. Here, a KC-135A (*right*) refuels another great Boeing aircraft, the B-52 Stratofortress.

first flight on July 15, 1954. Airlines all over the world realized that they would have to have this airplane—but no commercial orders came in.

The problem was purely financial. Most airlines had recently invested in new piston-engine equipment that had yet to pay for itself, and were thus unable to obtain financing for the new jet. Throughout the long, agonizing summer of 1954 it seemed Boeing might have made a colossal mistake, investing a fortune in an airplane no one could afford.

Help came swiftly, from two channels. One was an order by the USAF for 29 KC-135A jet tankers; the second was the magnificent gamble taken by Pan American Airways on October 13, 1955, when they ordered 20 Boeing 707s and 25 of the rival, look-a-like Douglas DC-8s. (In the event, Pan American would accept only 19 of the DC-8s, and would never buy another Douglas airliner.)

Pan Am began transatlantic jet service on October 26, 1958, with a 707 named the *Mayflower Clipper*, and nei-

ther Boeing nor the traveling world ever looked back.

The 707 won immediate acceptance, for it was a highly productive aircraft, capable of carrying up to 219 passengers at a cruising speed of 605 miles per hour. And while the 707 was intended for long-distance flight (its range was more than 3,600 miles), a design derivative, the 707-120, was adaptable to intermediate and short routes.

Like all the early jets, the 707 had some inherent drawbacks—noise and long stopping distances being the primary ones. Boeing solved both of these problems by spending $15,000,000 over seven years to develop a combination noise-suppressor/engine thrust reverser that cleared the way for a whole series of follow-on aircraft. The dominance of the 707 overshadowed the competition; the DC-8 never captured a similar share of the market and Convair's late entry, the 880, was a total commercial failure. The 707's success made it easier for Boeing to successfully produce and sell the 727s, 737s,

747s, 757s, and 767s of today, and, presumably, the 777s of tomorrow.

Other nations were entering the jet aviation picture at the same time as Britain and the United States. The Soviet Union had adapted a bomber to the passenger role to create the Tupelov Tu 104, but this was soon followed by a host of purpose-built designs for the world's largest airline, Aeroflot.

In France it was a time for glory under the leadership of President Charles de Gaulle, who had pulled his nation out of NATO, and was concentrating on building an independent nuclear striking force, the *force de frappe*. The Gallic spirit of independence encompassed civilian aviation as well. To de Gaulle, the issue was simple: Great nations build their own airliners, and France was a great nation. So it was that on May 27, 1955, one of the most beautiful and popular airliners in history, the Sud-Est Aviation SE-210 Caravelle, made its first flight.

The Caravelle had been designed to a specification calling for an aircraft capable of flying up to 1,300 miles at a block speed of 373 miles per hour, with 55 to 65 passengers. (Block speed is the average speed from take-off to landing, including climbs and descents; as such, it is a more valid method of judging speeds from the standpoint of carrying passengers and freight). The available power of contemporary jet engines caused Sud-Aviation (the name the company adopted in 1957) to design the Caravelle initially as a three-

The Sud-Aviation SE-210 Caravelle, shown here in a painting by John Batchelor. Comfortable and relatively quiet, the Caravelle was popular with passengers and crews alike. However, it was limited by a design that was lacking in "stretch" capability.

engine airliner, with the engines positioned at the tail, much as they were in the later Boeing 727. Subsequently, however, more powerful Rolls-Royce Avon engines became available, and the Caravelle evolved as the first airliner to have its two engines placed in the rear (this configuration would eventually appear on the Douglas DC-9).

There were sound aerodynamic and structural reasons for the engine placement: It left the wing clean and unencumbered by a pylon; a change in thrust had little effect upon the longitudinal stability of the aircraft; the risk of fire was reduced because the engines were located at a fairly safe distance from the fuel tanks; and perhaps most important of all, overall cabin noise was substantially reduced.

Because of the Comet disaster, the engineers at Sud-Aviation were especially careful in their rigorous testing of the Caravelle. "Fail-safe" engineering principles were applied extensively, because it was known that the routes flown by the Caravelle would require many take-offs and landings, and hence many cycles of the pressurization system. Cooperation between Sud-Aviation engineers and their counterparts at de Havilland and Rolls-Royce was considerable. So close was the cooperation, in fact, that the Caravelle's nose section was identical to that of the Comet; additionally, the cockpit layouts of the two planes were very similar.

The Caravelle soon proved itself to be perfectly suited for the shorter European routes, with its 460 mile–per–hour cruising speed and range of just over 1,000 miles. The Caravelle made history when 20 were purchased by United Airlines in 1960, the first foreign sale ever made to one of the "big four" American-based airlines (United, TWA, American, and Pan Am). The advent of the Caravelle on American routes was an important factor in spurring the development of both the Boeing 727 and the Douglas DC-9.

The Caravelle was well liked by both passengers and pilots; it had a very low accident rate and was easy to maintain. Like the Comet, however, the basic design did not have the built-in "stretch" capability that typified its Boeing counterparts. Consequently, the Caravelle was gradually withdrawn from service as younger, faster and more versitile competitors appeared on the scene.

Come Fly With Me!

Air travel was once almost exclusively the domain of the rich. So it was appropriate that, in the years immediately preceding World War II, a flight from San Francisco to Manila in the China Clipper, the lovely four-engine Martin M-130, was an elegant experience. The journey was slow, to be sure: a five-stop, 60-hour adventure, undertaken mostly at low altitudes over the Pacific Ocean and the islands that dotted its vast expanse. Yet there were pleasures to every journey, the chief among them being the reception accorded the passengers, who were greeted everywhere as celebrities.

Even into the 1950s, airplane travel remained the province of the well-to-do. A transcontinental journey in a propeller-driven Lockheed Constellation meant eight hours of relaxation, augmented by the presence of smiling, attentive stewardesses. The middle class traveled by rail, and the poor had to suffer the indignities of the bus.

The great increase in airline travel that occurred in the 1960s forever changed travel modes, converting airliners to airborne buses, and setting the once pristine airports ringing with bus-terminal bedlam. Airline fares became less and less expensive in relative terms to either rail or bus travel; in absolute terms, if one took into consideration the time involved in the trip, flying became a bargain, if no longer a pleasant one.

Airliner passengers, c.1950, display the happy faces of contented travelers.

The reason for this great "democratization" of air travel was the proliferation of highly productive jet aircraft, which forced airline executives to think of new ways to keep the seats filled.

The most obvious method was with canny manipulation of the cost of airline tickets. Over time, airline pricing has become an incredibly sophisticated system that separates the market into those who have to fly at certain times for business, and those who travel purely for pleasure. The first group pays through the nose for their tickets, while the others get some amazing bargains. (On the average airline trip, approximately 52 percent of the seats will be filled by passengers on business.)

This revolution is not restricted to the United States; flying is now routinely available to citizens of almost every country in the world, on a scale unheard of even 20 years ago. In 1970, there were 169,922,000 emplanements worldwide, for a total of 131,710,018,000 passenger miles. In 1990, there were 465,557,000 emplanements, for a total of 457,915,220,000 passenger miles. That's 465 *million* passenger miles in one year, with 600 million emplanements predicted for the year 2000! In America the figures for air travel are particularly impressive—78 percent of all men and 72 percent of all women have flown; 60 percent take more than one flight per year. The average American flyer takes 3.4 trips each year.

This onslaught has turned what used to be the tourist industry into the tourist terror. Millions of travelers from across the globe are crowding and sometimes even despoiling the sites they have flown to see. The sheer weight of numbers is staggering; tiny towns in England, for example, are inundated by summer tourists representing one thousand times their resident populations.

But no matter the commotion they cause, tourists bring dollars, yen, pounds, lira, francs, marks, and a myriad of other currencies to their host nations; and, as long as they continue to do so, the airlines will be there to haul them.

The eerie, otherwordly beauty of the F-117A is evident in this John Batchelor painting, which depicts a Stealth fighter launching an air-to-ground missile at an enemy target. In the opening minutes of the Persian Gulf War, Stealth fighters devastated Iraqi radar stations and other command and control facilities.

One sure way for an aircraft to earn its right to the title "classic" is in battle. In the 1991 Persian Gulf War, the Lockheed F-117A sneaked its way into classic status by repeatedly sneaking into the flak-filled skies over Baghdad to account for 95 percent of the Iraqi targets destroyed in that city. Stealth technology proved itself in impressive fashion.

"Stealth" is a relatively new buzz-word, but as a tactical concept, cam-ouflage of one sort or another has a familiar basis in nature. In human history, it goes back at least as far as primitive hunters, caped in the skins of a previous kill, stalking a herd of bison. In warfare, combatants have always tried to be stealthy—witness the Greek wooden horse at Troy; the creeping Birnam Wood intent upon the destruction of Macbeth; pirate ships flying false colors; Q-ships in World War I; and the massive elec-

Lockheed F-117A Stealth Fighter

The F-117A is the most startling—and effective—application of the stealth principle yet seen in warfare

tronic deception used by the Allies to mask the Normandy invasion in World War II.

The stealth concept has long been a part of aviation history. In 1917 German Zeppelins laden with bombs flew to England on moonless nights, shutting down their engines to drift silently over London. The Germans also experimented with a Linke-Hoffman bomber during the Great War, covering it in part with celluloid

only to find that the material reflected more light than regular paint. In World War II, the most significant stealth breakthrough was "window," strips of aluminum foil British bombers dropped to blank out enemy radar. In the United States the "Yehudi" experiment demonstrated that special lighting could be installed on a B-24 Liberator bomber so that in certain conditions of haze it would disappear from visual contact.

Lockheed's F-117A, then, is part of a venerable tradition of military stealth. Ironically, the fighter's first stealthy achievement was bureaucratic: It was kept secret and literally hidden for a several years by the U.S. military, who removed it from the eyes of a U.S. public ravenous for information about new weapons. Despite the persistent rumors of "weird" aircraft operating at night out of the USAF base at Tonopah,

LOCKHEED F-117A STEALTH FIGHTER

Nevada, the Department of Defense denied all knowledge of the aircraft, and no information was released. But the strain of intensive night operations, compounded by the burden of continual separation from families, placed enormous stress on the pilots. Numerous pilot complaints of fatigue and spatial disorientation may have presaged a pair of fatal F-117A crashes that occured in the area.

When official information about the aircraft was finally released, the aviation world was rocked—here was a totally new (and peculiar-looking) first-line fighter, from the company that had produced the beautiful P-38 Lightning, Constellation, U-2, and SR-71 Blackbird. Pundits in the press immediately took a hatchet to the F-117A program, not for the plane's appearance, but because the program was incredibly expensive: $111.2 million per aircraft. The status of the F-117A was not enhanced when over-optimistic claims were made about its accuracy when it was used on December 20, 1989, during *Operation Just Cause*—the invasion of Panama.

But all doubts were put to rest in the first blinding American air attacks on Baghdad in January 1991, when F-117As penetrated the formidable Iraqi Air Defense System with surgical precision to devastate Iraq's command and control infrastructure.

Using GBU-24 laser-guided glide bombs, the F-117As took out a wide variety of targets. Many of the most dramatic strikes were captured on videotape: Iraqi Air Force headquarters took a bomb hit in the center of its roof, and the air defense headquarters was struck by a bomb that plummeted down a ventilation shaft, exploding with such force that the building's airlock door was blown out. Other F-117A targets included hardened aircraft shelters, air defense systems, and sites related to nuclear, biological, and chemical warfare. The F-117As ranged with impunity through the Baghdad skies, untouched by a firestorm of flak that surrounded them.

The F-117A performed with incredible precision, clearing the way for other aircraft to hit their targets. And in some instances, when the enemy defenses were simply too tough for

Precursor to the F-117A, the Northrop XB-35 Flying Wing was a failure that led to better things. In *B-35A's In Action Over Hokkaido - 1946*, William P. Yenne envisioned the use of Flying Wings in a prolonged Pacific war.

the F-16s or FB-111s to penetrate, the F-117A was called on to do the job.

As the war progressed, it was obvious that the F-117A was also a reliable aircraft, relatively easy to service and "turn around" quickly. And no Stealth planes were lost during the war, another indicator of their reliability, as well as the skill of their pilots and crews.

With success came the perception that the F-117A was no longer ugly, but beautiful; as the functional reasons underlying the aircraft's unusual planform (the top view of a three-view aircraft drawing) and angular construction became apparent, the F-117A acquired an internal cohesion that made the plane seem artful.

Just how does the Stealth "work?" Before we can understand the ways in which an aircraft becomes stealthy, it is necessary to understand a little bit about radar. A radar set used for detecting aircraft transmits a beam of energy, usually in a pattern which scans a defined sector of the sky. The effectiveness of the radar set in detecting an aircraft depends upon the strength of its signal, the amount of that strength reflected back by the target aircraft, the amount of the power reflected back that is gathered in by the radar's antenna, and the length of time that the radar is trained on the target.

Knowing this, designers of stealth aircraft attempt to minimize the elements they can control—the amount of reflected radar energy, and the length of time that the radar can be kept trained on the target.

Lockheed was long fortunate in having the services of Kelly Johnson, the company's renown chief of Advanced Development Projects, (or "Skunk Works," to use its popular nickname); and it was twice blessed in that Johnson's successor was Ben Rich, a man less well known than Johnson, but of similar incisive genius. Rich directed his team to minimize both of the controllable elements by reducing the F-117A's radar cross section (RCS), adding radar-absorbent materials (RAM), and trapping radar energy with specially designed RAM structural components known as corner reflectors. Essentially, the aircraft's exterior surfaces would be flat and faceted, always at angles greater than 30 degrees, so that radar energy directed against them would not be returned to the radar's antennae.

And just as the individual elements of the exterior were designed to minimize radar return, so were the major lines of the aircraft itself—the wing and tail had straight leading edges, and the undersurface was completely flat.

Underneath the plates of RAM, which are attached to the airframe by epoxy adhesive, the F-117 is of relatively conventional aluminum construction. Rich's design team paid close attention to detail, so that all antennas are either flush, retractable, or removable. The engine inlets have screens to reduce the return from the engine compressor face.

The cockpit cavity is one of the largest radar reflectors on most fighters, and in the F-117A care has been taken to reduce this as much as possible. The angular, visor-like canopy has dog-tooth edges which overlap the primary structure to seal out energy from radar. For additional protection, the laminated cockpit windows have a gold-film layer that absorbs radar impulses instead of reflecting them.

The wing, aside from its unusual shape, is of conventional construction, using elevons for pitch and roll control (very much in the manner of the classic Northrop Flying Wing of the late 1940s). Perhaps the most unusual aspect of the F-117A's blended wing/body arrangement is the way that each of the two General Electric F404-GE-F1D2 engines are provided with 12 flattened exhaust nozzles along the trailing edge, between the two huge flaps. The exhaust is emitted against the flattened tail section, which is covered with heat-absorbing tiles similar to those used on the Space Shuttle, once again to minimize the aircraft's infrared signature. The sharply swept V-type tail surfaces give a distinctive swallow-tailed look to the F-117A.

Despite early press reports that the F-117A was difficult to fly (which inspired the nickname, "the Wobblin' Goblin"), pilots of the 37th Tactical Fighter Wing report it to be quite pleasant in the air—especially when it is shielding them in combat.

Although it might seem otherwise, the F-117A had been preceded by a similar, smaller test aircraft in a project codenamed "Have Blue"; the F-117A project was coded "Senior Trend," although the popular name "Nighthawk" is associated with it now.

The F-117A has a high performance that its looks belie. Top speed is about 600 miles per hour (.90 Mach), although the airplane is sup-

Above: Side view of an F-117A in flight, with the engine exhaust nozzles clearly visible along the trailing edge of the wing.

Above: Front view of the Stealth fighter.
Right: The F-117A's cockpit canopy features dog-tooth edging and coated windscreen capable of absorbing radar.

An F-117A is refueled in flight by a KC-10 tanker. The Stealth's maximum range on internal fuel is a relatively short 1,250 miles, which means that aerial refueling operations are a routine part of most missions.

A walled revetment on a Saudi airstrip protects an F-117A from attack during the Persian Gulf War. That such attacks never materialized is due in large measure to the successful use of Stealth fighters in the conflict.

posedly capable of attaining supersonic speeds in a dive. The maximum range on internal fuel is 1,250 miles, and the aircraft is fitted with a boom-type aerial refueling receptacle. The plane has a wingspan of 43 feet, four inches; overall length is 65 feet, 11 inches, and it stands to a height of 12 feet, five inches. Maximum take-off weight is 52,500 pounds.

The lay observer who sees the Lockheed F-117A and America's other "stealthy" aircraft, the Northrop B-2 bomber, side-by-side is bound to wonder why the two planes are so different in appearance. The fact is that in the 1970s technology developed by Lockheed, the F-117A's faceted flatplate design was the best available solution to the stealth problem. The bomber, with its requirement for a very long range at high subsonic cruising speeds, simply couldn't afford the drag that faceting causes. The Northrop company's long history with the flying wing configuration proved fortuitous, for a flying wing has a natural low radar cross section. Thus the wing shape selected for the B-2 was completely different from the F-117A's. Still, the Stealth fighter is more than just a collection of sharp angles. From above, it is all straight lines, with a saw-tooth trailing edge, but from the side

it is smoothly, almost sensuously curved.

When Lockheed and Northrop were placed in competition for the upcoming Advanced Tactical Fighter, the Northrop entrant, the YF-23, very much resembled the B-2, while Lockheed's YF-22 was a far more elegant aircraft than the F-117A. Yet both had stealthy characteristics, and in the end it was the Lockheed proposal that won, a tribute to the YF-22's maneuverability and to the confidence the Department of Defense has in the firm that created the F-117A.

In the warm afterglow of the Gulf War, there have been calls for the production of additional F-117As to supplement the original order of 59 aircraft. Although more F-117As are probably not in the cards, it is almost certain that the aircraft that replaces the canceled A-12 will draw heavily on the lessons taught by the Stealth fighter in the skies over Baghdad.

In the competition to build a replacement for the F-117A, Lockheed's YF-22 (*top*) has emerged a clear winner over the Northrop YF-23 (*middle*). America's other stealth plane, the Northrop B-2 (*above*), resembles its predecessor, the XB-35, in outline only.